Somebody's Daughter

Zara H. Phillips began her professional career working as a backing vocalist for Sir Bob Geldof when he recruited her for his first solo projects after he departed the chart-topping UK band The Boomtown Rats. Zara's musical career quickly blossomed from that point, as she continued her work on tour, in television and videos with UK artists such as Matt Bianco, Nick Kamen, David Essex, Bananarama and the solo project from Dire Straits' John Illsley.

Born and raised in London, Zara loved to sing and dance from a young age and enjoyed spending hours in her room writing all the lyrics to musicals and performing each part. Zara moved to Los Angeles in 1996 where she continued writing new songs and performing solo. In 2005, Zara finished work on a new CD entitled 'When the Rain Stops', produced by Grammy award winner Ted Perlman.

In 2008, Zara finished directing and producing an adoption documentary entitled 'ROOTS: UNKNOWN', which focussed on the emotional influence adoption has on the adoptee and their families. The film won Best Homegrown Documentary at The Garden State Film festival in New Jersey. This led to her writing her first book, 'Mother Me' published by BAAF (British Association for Adoption and Fostering) in March 2008 described by Sir Bob Geldof as a 'brave and compelling book'.

In 2009, Zara co-wrote a song and made a video with Darryl McDaniels from RUNDMC called 'I'm Legit' to raise awareness on the emotional impact of adoption and the importance of birth records (which are closed in many States in the USA.) The video has been used to help educate congressmen and the general public on the issue.

In 2013, Zara debuted her one woman show, 'Beneath My Father's Sky', centred around her relationship with her adoptive father, and it won the award for Best Direction in the United Solo Festival in New York. The show has since been performed in Los Angeles, San Francisco and New Jersey, and in 2016 it was performed at 'Upstairs at The Gatehouse' in London. Zara writes articles for various adoption magazines, regularly talks and facilitates workshops and events related to adoption issues, and still performs her music at clubs in NYC and New Jersey.

www.zaraphillips.net

Zara H. Phillips

Somebody's Daughter

A moving journey of discovery,
recovery and adoption

JOHN BLAKE

Published by John Blake Publishing,
3 Bramber Court, 2 Bramber Road,
London W14 9PB, England

www.johnblakebooks.com

www.facebook.com/johnblakebooks [f]
twitter.com/jblakebooks [t]

This edition published in 2018

ISBN: 978 1 78606 566 7

British Library Cataloguing-in-Publication Data:

A catalogue record for this book is available from the British Library.

Design by www.envydesign.co.uk

Printed and bound in Great Britain by Clays Ltd, St Ives plc

1 3 5 7 9 10 8 6 4 2

Papers used by John Blake Publishing are natural, recyclable products
made from wood grown in sustainable forests. The manufacturing processes conform
to the environmental regulations of the country of origin.

Every attempt has been made to contact the relevant copyright-holders,
but some were unobtainable. We would be grateful if the appropriate
people could contact us.

John Blake Publishing is an imprint of Bonnier Publishing
www.bonnierpublishing.com

For all the babies that have been separated
from their mothers

Contents

'What hurts you, blesses you. Darkness is your candle.'
JALALUDDIN MEYLANA RUMI

Foreword

My first encounter with Zara was on a talk show I was presenting. She was a guest, sitting there in the audience, making sense. It's a rare talent and my God we could do with more of it in the world. We talked after and had a mutual check list that fellow adoptees play swapsies with. It's a kind of inventory of feelings. 'Got. Got. Got. You feel like that too?'

When you meet and talk to another adopted person you realise you are both, in one sense, lost children. We are always forever more amen in perpetuity adopted 'children'. Our status and feelings are frozen in time and limited by our own insecurities and need to belong. This might not completely define us – I am defined as much by the wonderful adoption and amazing family that I have – but it is a key ingredient in the whole mess of who we are or who we think we are. The inextricable tangle of who we are.

When I met Zara I felt this. And this beautiful person, in the words of the song 'took my letters and read them all out loud'. She articulates – no delete that, articulate sounds too stuffy and formal – she expresses beautifully what so many children like us feel.

My odyssey into the part of me I didn't know but needed to understand – tracing and meeting my birth mother and then birth father – was driven first and foremost by just that. I needed to lay the demons to rest and get on with the rest of my life, free of the questions and doubts. I hope this isn't self-pity, it's self-knowledge.

Not that I've reached some state of Zen-like inner peace – that wouldn't be at all good for the creative process ☺ – but it's a hell of a lot better than it was before. You don't realise how much you need to do it for your own well-being until you do it.

Zara's feelings will be recognised by every adopted person on the block. When you walk through that door though, you need full body armour before you come through. It's a brand new past, a whole new future and boy does it takes guts, strength and support to get there; to handle it all. In retrospect, I needed much more of the latter but the more people talk and write as powerfully as this, the better for all us children. We just want to play in peace. We just want to play.

Nicky Campbell
January 2018

Author's Note

Once I received the news that this book was going to be published I was excited but incredibly nervous. I was reminded once more that when one tells the truth about their own story, others will be involved who may have strong feelings about it. I tried to explain to the people I had close relationships with that the focus of this story is mine, that it is written purely from the inner journey of the adoptee. It caused some very difficult, hard conversations. Scared I would lose people that I love, I almost abandoned the whole project. Was I being selfish for telling my truth? Why was I so compelled to go deeper into myself and reveal some very personal things about my life? I didn't really have the answers. For a long time, all I knew was I needed to share the truth of my journey. Maybe it's my way of making sense of something that often feels so complicated. For so many years I never had a voice. I lived in silence, I never shared my secret with anyone: the secret of my truth, the truth of my pain, my endless heartache, loss and grief – after all, aren't us adoptees supposed to feel grateful?

Over the years as I have been asked to share my experience with adopted families I realised that even though a lot has changed in terms of things being talked about, one thing remains the same: there is still a huge silence about the emotional impact adoption causes. Meanwhile many adopted people struggle with their lives. They are over represented in treatment centres and institutions. Some are unable to tell their parents the truth of how they feel in case they hurt them; adopted parents still battle to understand their children's behaviour. Some shame still lingers that we cannot solve this alone.

I was encouraged to tell the truth so that my story may help others. As I talked it over with my friends and agent, Adrian, it became clearer to me. If I hold back, I'm still doing that little baby adoptee a disservice and therefore I decided to write this book based on as much truth as I feel people can accept and handle. I have changed names and combined situations that I have been through to protect people. The purpose of this book is for the reader to understand the inner journey and my hope is that anyone connected with adoption, addiction or grief in their life may find that my experience resonates with them. So here it is…

Introduction

Newark Penn Station, New Jersey,
August 2016

There's traffic as I approach the station and I'm worried that I'll be late. All I have to do is turn the corner and I'll be there. I'm still not that familiar with Newark Penn Station in New Jersey, although I should be – I've lived here for eleven years. 'Eleven years,' I find myself saying out loud. So much has happened that no one could ever have imagined.

The car in front of me moves slowly but I know I won't make the green light. I consider beeping but restrain myself. Instead I count how many cars are ahead of me; maybe next it will be my turn. The sky is darkening. The wind picks up and it begins to rain. I slowly move forward again, this time barely making the green. I turn towards the main station, pulling my car into the first opening I see.

Somebody's Daughter

I text Michelle: 'I'm here, black car. No rush, excited.'

A moment later my phone beeps: 'Coming, yay!'

I open my car door, aware that I may need to move it any second if a cop comes. The wind picks up again. My hair is now tousled all around, as I scan the faces in the crowd. And then I see her waving to me: a tall, slim blonde woman, her long hair blowing about in the wind, her scarf blowing around her. I wave back and she hurries across the street.

We are both smiling as we hug. I open the boot, put her bag in and we get in the car, laughing a little as we try to get warm.

'So,' she says excitedly, 'did he call?'

'He did,' I reply. 'I said we'd call him when we were close by and that we'd start heading towards him.'

'I'm so relieved.' Her voice had a similar tone to mine, it was just our accents that were different: her's a straight American and mine British.

I glance at her for a moment. We had Skyped, and met briefly just once before, but this was the first time we would be spending the day together. We were two years apart, Michelle just turning fifty and me almost fifty-two. My birthday was three days after her's. I see myself in her face, although she has light blue eyes and mine are green.

'Our teeth,' I say as she looks at me, 'we have the same teeth.' And she laughs her light, airy laugh. I like her energy; she is upbeat and full of fun.

'Balloons?' I ask.

'Oh yes,' she replies, 'definitely balloons.'

I start driving; the rain is coming down a little heavier.

Michelle dials a number into her phone.

'Hello, could we order some balloons to go? Do you have one with "It's a girl"? Fabulous, we'll be there in half an hour.'

I can't help laughing.

'I'm so glad we have the same sense of humour,' she says, tilting her head back with a loud throaty laugh, and picks up her phone again. She mouths to me, 'I'm calling to tell him we're almost there.'

'Hello,' she says playfully. 'Yes, it's us, we're on our way… about forty-five minutes. See you there, in Dunkin' Donuts? Of course, that's our special place after all.'

We make eye contact, both of us beaming. It was surreal, quite a story, we had said, repeating it over and over. Yet sitting next to this woman who I only recently knew existed felt so comfortable. I feel like I've known her forever.

We find the balloon shop and run in, seeing our display waiting, making us laugh out loud again like two teenage girls. We ask a young man nearby to take our photo. Standing side by side, with the rain still coming down, we hold onto our balloons as they sway.

He looks at us with a question in his eyes but says nothing.

'Thank you,' I shout back from our car. 'I know that

must have looked weird with the balloons, but it's a long story. She's my sister.'

Michelle lets out her loud laugh again as we get in the car. Talking the whole time, we drive to where he is waiting for us.

1

London, 1987

'My name is Zara and I'm here because I have been dealing with my brother and his heroin addiction. He went into treatment and I went to family groups, but it was suggested that I come here.'

I notice how full the church basement is, a pungent smell that might come from the tramp-like man sat in the corner, sipping his tea. I see a few women amongst the male-dominated group. An attractive lady gives me a warm smile, which encourages me to keep talking.

'I might be an addict myself,' I continue hesitantly. 'But quite honestly, it's my brother that has a problem. I am not sure if I have a problem with alcohol, as really, if you gave me drugs, I much prefer those. The alcohol was just a top-up, you know, to give it more of a hit.'

Somebody's Daughter

I inhale my cigarette, aware that all eyes are on me. Feeling my face burn red, I stop talking. There were some chortles from the crowd as I had spoken and a shuffling in their seats.

I was twenty-two. I hadn't done what half these other people had done in their lives, but I had already packed in quite a lot of experience, that I couldn't deny.

'Hello and welcome, keep coming back,' the group chants in unison, the thick smoke filling up the room. As the meeting ends, I light up another cigarette, unsure of who to talk to.

'Hello,' a thick Scottish accent says next to me. It was the man that had been sitting two chairs away from me. I turn to look at him now, noticing his kind, open face. He shakes my hand.

'My name is James,' he says. 'Welcome.'

I smile a little cautiously and find myself repeating, 'I'm not sure if I really am an addict myself. It's my brother, you see. He was a heroin addict. I don't take heroin – well, maybe I took it once…' I pause. 'Okay, maybe twice.'

I was aware of how nuts I was beginning to sound. But James just smiles.

'Why don't you come to the Spaghetti House? Me and my mate Terry will be there,' he suggests.

I surprise myself by saying yes and follow them out of the church into the cool summer evening, across the street and into a small but busy restaurant. I sit opposite them as we order some tea and food. Their eyes are shiny, they smile a lot; they seem happy. I'm nervous sitting with these men, yet somehow comfortable at the same time.

'So, Zara, how long have you been sober?' asks James.

'Oh, well, I'm not really here to stay sober, as I don't have that much of a problem. Like I said, it's my brother – he went to treatment for heroin addiction. I don't do that.'

The waitress takes our food order; James is playful with her, cheeky.

'Oh,' he says, turning back to me. 'So, you're just here to check us out?'

'Well…' I say, playing with the packets of sugar on the table, aware that my face is turning red again. 'It was suggested that I come. Some people are worried about me.'

'Worried?' he says. 'Do you think they have reason to be?'

'Not really. I mean, I do smoke pot to help me sleep, but who doesn't? I really love cocaine but I know loads of people that take it. I just feel depressed a lot and it helps.'

Why am I telling these people the truth? I ask myself.

'What do you love about cocaine?' James asks.

'It makes me feel exactly how I want to feel. It gives me confidence,' I reply honestly, almost getting a body rush as I talk about it. 'I'm not good with people and situations. So, I don't know…' My voice trails off. 'I'm not an addict,

addict, if you know what I mean. It just makes me feel more confident.'

'Do you drink at all?' he asks gently.

'I'm not an alcoholic…' My voice is sounding edgy. 'I'm not like those men in the meeting, I just use alcohol to get more of a buzz after I've taken cocaine. I'm a backing singer, so of course I drink on the road. It's hard to get drugs there. But before that, I just had one or two drinks to give me the feeling.'

They both nod, smiling slightly. James leans in; I notice his receding hairline and how blue his sparkling eyes are. I'm beginning to feel trapped in the booth; I want to escape, yet I don't move.

'The feeling…' He bursts out laughing, winking at Terry. 'The feeling,' he says again and I know my face is reddening. 'Do you think normal drinkers do that?' he asks.

At this I fall silent and stop twirling my spaghetti as I feel my eyes welling up a little. 'I don't know what normal people do, I don't think about that.' I can hear my own anger.

'Do you steal?' Terry asks. My body stiffens. 'For drugs, I mean, do you steal? Do you lie to friends and family about how much you use?' he continues matter-of-factly.

'Blimey, that's a bit personal, isn't it?' I try to laugh it off but neither of them are smiling. 'Well, no, I don't share my drugs. If my friends knew I had cocaine they would want it all. Does that make me a bad person? But why would I? It's expensive. I'm great at stealing make-up and clothes – I do that all the time. I know it's wrong, I haven't done that for ages.' I half-laugh again and quickly add, 'But I've stolen for friends so it's not like it's just for me.'

I wish I would stop talking, but it seems easy with them and, in a strange way, a relief. They stop smiling; I'm not good with silence.

'Do I steal for drugs? Do you mean do I try and get guys to give me drugs for free?' I try to sound light-hearted. They both nod.

'Of course!' My voice is animated again. 'Isn't that the beauty of being a girl? Can we order tea?' I know I'm changing the subject, but I feel I still need to explain. 'Look, I'm not a prostitute. I don't have to have sex with them unless I really want to. Maybe I kissed a guy for blow [cocaine] and led him to believe he would get more, but I'm great at escaping, I always have been – Houdini is my middle name. And my boyfriend now, well, that's different – he actually gave me cocaine for free.' I pause. 'Well, he did, but now he charges me. What a nerve!'

'Do you think all young woman behave like this?' James asks casually.

'I don't fucking know,' I say, beginning to feel angry. 'And quite honestly, I don't really care. What's normal anyway?'

'Well, my question is,' says Terry, pushing back his dark hair. 'Is your life working for you?'

Somebody's Daughter

I can't look at either of them. I can feel their eyes on me, and I know they're seeing me. How can I explain it all – the constant anxiety and paranoia, the feeling of hopelessness and sadness? I had always felt that my heart was broken and I was tired; I was surviving day-to-day, I knew.

I shrug my shoulders. 'I suppose not.' I say quietly, unable to hide the irritation in my voice.

'Why don't you just try and stop and see what happens? Come to some of these meetings and if you don't like it, we'll gladly hand all your misery back to you.' James looks me in the eye and says it with such kindness.

I don't respond for a moment, my gaze wandering to the back of the restaurant, noticing others from the meeting smiling and laughing loudly, their voices full of expression.

'Why would you care whether I do or I don't? What's it really to you?'

'Ooh,' James turns to Terry. 'She's an angry one, isn't she?'

'It doesn't make any difference to us what you do,' Terry replies. 'But I have a feeling it could for you. If you just give it a go, things will change, I can promise you that. You don't have anything to lose.'

'I don't know that I can do that,' I whisper. 'I need them, I need the drugs to help me.'

'Help with what?' he says softly.

'Live,' I explain.

16

'Honey, you're not going to live if you keep this up, now are you? And that fruit salad that you seem to be enjoying is full of alcohol.'

I place the bowl down on the table.

'No, it isn't,' I protest, perhaps too defensively.

'Excuse me, lovely,' he says to the pretty waitress. 'Is there alcohol in the fruit salad?'

'Of course,' she smiles, 'smothered in it.'

'Oh, bloody hell! Now you're telling me I can't eat a simple fruit salad with a tiny bit of alcohol?' They're seriously pissing me off, and why do they keep smiling?

'Eat it?' Terry responds in a dry tone. 'I think you inhaled it.' I walk slowly back to the Tube into the night. I have both their numbers written down carefully and a small glimmer of hope.

* * *

I don't call either of them for a while – I'm not ready. I go back out on the road as a backing singer. The touring and the travelling keep me from thinking too much. But as I lay one night in the hotel bed, my married lover sleeping next to me, I feel the walls collapsing around me. I'm not sure how much more I can take of feeling the way that I do.

That evening, as I arrive back in London I don't go home. Instead I go to meet Stan – 'Stan the little Buddha man' as we all liked to call him. I'd met Stan when I first went to a 12-step meeting. For some reason he seemed to take an interest in me and showed me a lot of kindness but I didn't want to hear it at the time. As I kept telling myself, I wasn't an addict, it was everyone else around me.

Seeing my face and knowing me the way he does, he looks at me directly. He doesn't hide the concern in his eyes.

'Zara, you are twenty-two but I'm afraid you're not going to make it to twenty-three.'

I feel like I've just been kicked in the solar plexus. My body starts to shake. I know he's right and I also know that I can't stop by myself.

It's 30 August 1987. The air has started to cool as autumn approaches. I wander the streets buying packets of chocolate, filling my mouth so that I can barely breathe, smothering every emotion that tries to surface. I go home, find my stash of weed and smoke a little. Looking out of the curtain-less windows, the moon looks extra-bright. I think about a story I heard recently at an AA meeting, where a young woman whose life had been so out of control was celebrating four years of sobriety. She was expecting her first child. I thought about her tears of joy, her talk of this newfound freedom; she was happy. I'd been riveted by her every word. I wanted what she had – I just didn't see how for me it could be possible. I knew the drugs had won. Every day I thought about them, wondering where I was going to get them. Every day I was spinning out of control, a weight and sadness pulling on me.

Turning onto my knees, kneeling on the mattress on the floor, I hear myself say, 'I have no clue if anyone exists up there, but I'm in serious trouble. I need some help.'

The moon appears to shine brightly on me. I lie still, watching its white light shine a path through my window into the room. As I feel a warmth and calmness enveloping me, I wonder if it's the drug in my system but it feels so powerful that I don't want to move. As I finally fall into a deep sleep I know that something has changed in me; I can't put it into words but I feel hope. When I wake up the next morning the first thing I do is call James.

'I'm ready,' I say. 'I'm ready, tell me what I need to do.'

2

London, 1977

When I was young I used to slide my body against the corridor wall in the darkness to see if I could reach the door to my bedroom without turning the light on. My father would get so angry if the corridor light was left on, screaming at the top of his voice, 'Turn off that bloody light! Do you know how big my lighting bill is?'

So I'd slink like a snake against the cold wall, counting the pictures that I bumped into, counting them all as I went to help me gauge how close I was to my room. If I even turned on the light for a second and he was in one of those moods he would fling open the door angrily and I would run. I was slight and nimble, used to darting out the way, unlike him. My father was so overweight, I didn't recognise him as the same slim man from the photo of his younger self. Puffing and panting, snorting after me, his curly hair wet with sweat… I would giggle each time he tried to catch me. I always made it to my bedroom, closing the door on him, leaning against it to make it hard to open. He might have been overweight, but he was weak.

'Zara, you need to respect me. Do you hear me?' he would shout in his harsh judge's voice.

I stayed quiet, thinking about respect. I might have been young, but I knew that it wasn't something I could ever feel towards a man that treated me this way. If he wanted my respect, he wouldn't get it by shouting. My father, however, wasn't going to make me feel bad that night, because I had a delicious secret, a secret that convinced me that life really could feel good at times. No one was going to spoil that.

* * *

Last night I was at my best friend's brother's bar mitzvah – she seemed to have invited the whole school, there were so many children there. And I danced with David. A tall boy, with brown hair, olive skin and kind deep brown eyes, he is almost a year older than me

'I'm fourteen and a half,' he tells me proudly.

Taking my hand, he pulls me gently away from the party and down the pathway to the garden. It's a little cold out but I'm still warm from dancing.

Halfway down the path we stop. Taking my face in his hands, he kisses me gently on the lips, and then slowly I feel his tongue pushing into my mouth. I have my eyes open the whole time. I wonder if he can tell I've never been kissed before.

'I'm roasting hot,' I say, as I lay back on the damp grass.

'This will cool us down, lie next to me.'

I can feel the warmth of his body as our shoulders touch.

'That's a red dwarf star,' says David as he points upwards into the clear night sky. 'Can you see it? It's smaller than the others. Doesn't burn as much so lives for ages, it actually stops the other stars from shining brighter.'

'It does?' I'm impressed. 'That's a bit mean, though – everyone should be allowed to shine as bright as they want.' He laughs playfully.

'You're cute,' he says.

I instantly blush, glad that he can't see me in the darkness.

'Isn't it amazing,' I whisper to him, 'that everyone in the whole world lives under the same sky, seeing the same moon?'

'I've never really thought about that,' he replies honestly, propping himself up next to me.

'I think about it all the time,' I whisper. I can feel him looking at me.

'Why do you think about that?' he asks.

I decide to reveal my secret, something I rarely tell anyone.

'My mother... Well, my first mother, she had to give

me away. I think about her looking at the sky, seeing the stars and the moon… I think about her a lot.' I stretch out, touching David's hand.

'Do you think she does?' I ask him.

'Look at the sky? Of course, she must,' he replies.

'I like to imagine that,' I say. 'It makes me feel closer to her,' Feeling self-conscious, I turn towards him and I ask urgently, 'Is that silly?'

He lays there silently for a moment and then says, 'No, it's not silly, but what about your father?'

'Father?' I'm truly surprised. 'I don't have a father, I only have a teenage mother – that's what they told me. A mother who couldn't take care of me, living under the same sky. No one has ever mentioned a father before.'

'Zara, everyone has a father.' He sits right up then, looking down at me. A wave of embarrassment washes over me.

'Let's go and dance now. Do you want to?' I say quickly, desperate to change the subject as he takes my hand and leads me back inside.

I feel like I've been lifted out of a giant dark cave into the brightest hopeful light. Here I am, just been kissed for the first time. More thrilling than that was the fact that I had another father out there. Very probably a kind, gentle father, because if I were really his child, whoever that man was, maybe he would love me; he would think I was pretty and tell me so occasionally. I would sit on his lap laughing and cuddling him, because that's what fathers and daughters did. I'd seen it so many times on television and in all the movies: all daddies loved their own little girls.

And so my adopted father's anger did not scare me. I knew now why he couldn't play with me and cuddle me. It was because I wasn't really his, and he didn't understand me in the way a natural father would.

I felt dizzy with excitement at this new knowledge. Later that night, as my dad stares at the ground, ignoring me talking to him, not raising his eyes to look at me as he's done for years, I actually feel sorry for him. After all, I have another father – another father out there, somewhere, living under this huge sky. And I knew for a fact that my father that lived in this house didn't have another daughter.

Poor him, I thought as I closed my eyes that night, *poor, poor him*.

* * *

There are many children in our street to play with, but my favourite of all is one little girl, Cassie, who is the same age as me. She lives in a big brick house facing my family's home in our cul-de-sac with her older sister and brother. I admire her sassy smile, the way she wiggles her hips as she walks and her swimsuit, pink and shimmery, with flower holes cut out at the side. She let me try it on once and I felt like a queen as I paraded in front of her.

Somebody's Daughter

One afternoon, when we were about eight years old, she and I were sitting on the hot steps that led up to my front door, licking ice lollies. My mother in her pale blue summer dress, covering her shapely body, was lovingly fussing around us with paper napkins to protect our clothes as they melted in the warm sun.

'Lick them as fast as you can,' she said smiling, as she walked back inside the house

Watching my mother go, I whisper secretively to Cassie, 'How were you borned?'

'Borned?' she says, a little unsure at first as to what I mean.

'Yes, borned. When you were a baby, a borned baby, what was your story?' I ask, looking directly at her face.

'Oh well, my story is simply spectacular…' Cassie pauses, pushing back her dark hair with her sticky fingers and taking a deep breath she begins, speaking very proudly, 'First, I rode on the back of a horse that could fly, to a place…' She stops momentarily. 'I forget what it was called, some magical place. There was a princess, I know, there was definitely a princess who came to meet us. She picked me up and placed me in my Mummy's tummy so I would finish growing.' Another lick of her lolly. 'She then gave my daddy a special feather from a golden bird that she had tucked in her pocket. It was a lucky feather and then they just waited and waited.'

My eyes grew wider with wonder as my ice lolly melted down my hands. Licking a red blob off my wrist, I looked at her, wanting her to continue.

'After they waited a few days or weeks, I was borned.' She is smiling now, the red lolly around her lips, her hands spread wide dramatically as she continues, 'They all came and bought me presents, so many that they filled the whole room. My bubba, my grandpa, Mummy and Daddy, all cried and cried.'

'Why did they cry?' I ask, a little worriedly.

'Because they were happy, silly! When babies are born people are happy and they cry happy tears.' She licks some more. 'How were you borned?'

Sucking the lolly stick, silent now, then chewing the end of the wood and thinking about her story – the princess, the tears – I speak softly.

'I wasn't borned, I was chosen,' I say seriously.

'*Chosen*?' Cassie's eyes grow wide with interest.

'Yes, chosen. There was a room full of babies all lined up in their cots.'

'Like a shop?' she says curiously.

'Yes, I think so. The mummies and daddies walked along looking at each one, deciding if they liked them, whether they wanted a boy or a girl, a fat baby or a small one. I was the last one left in the Jewish baby home.'

'How do you know you were the last baby?' Cassie asks.

'Because my mummy told me,' I reply.

'How could you be chosen then if you were the last one?'

I sit silently, my mind trying to make sense of what she has just said.

'Cassie, I was chosen, my mummy told me.' I feel tearful.

She links her little arm around me comfortingly. 'Of course it doesn't matter how we were borned,' she says, her voice loud and high, emphasising the word 'borned'. 'Shall we pretend forever that we are sisters?' she asks softly.

We start laughing loudly, leaning back on the hot steps and giggling in the way only best friends can. In those small moments I felt so much hope.

* * *

I'm a secretive little girl, I know. I can't seem to help myself or give my mother what she wants.

'My mother and I were always so close,' my mother says again to me, teasing her blonde hairsprayed do. 'We did everything together, she was my best friend.'

I stand at her bedroom door, feeling the shame wash over me, along with the knowledge that I'm not what she wants in a daughter.

'Did I ever tell you,' she continues, gazing at her own reflection in the mirror, 'that my mother died in February, the month you were conceived?'

I nod my head. She has told me this many times.

'Isn't it strange that she died as you were conceived?' Pausing, she fluffs the back of her hair in the mirror. 'You're like her in many ways. You have the same mannerisms, but of course you couldn't have got them from her, you must copy things from me. But it's strange that she died as you were conceived, isn't it?' She is looking at me now as she turns to slip on her shoes.

She has rarely said the word adopted, it's a word she seems to avoid. She did her duty as was suggested by the social services by reading me a children's book on adoption. I have never forgotten that book – I still see the pictures of the adopted parents so clearly in my mind, peering through the crib at a little baby, saying he was 'far too serious' for them, that they would prefer to wait for a different baby, a 'happier' one. Are any babies whose mothers have just relinquished them happy? That was how my mother told me I was adopted, but what she doesn't know is that I still cry for that illustrated serious baby.

I know she wants me to say something, but I can't speak. I know what she's insinuating – she wants me to agree that we are similar, that I'm like her. She wants something from me; she wants me to say her belief out loud that maybe I did trade souls with her mother as she passed and I was conceived but I can't give her that reassurance because it hurts too much that she is so desperate for us to connect.

Somebody's Daughter

I'm silent, always silent, so my mother says frustratedly. It's not that I don't think or feel, it's all there, trapped inside. I feel like someone could cut a hole in the top of my head and they would spray into the room, filling it to the brim – I always wonder if it's the same for everyone else.

As my mother looks at me, I see the hurt in her eyes. My guilt and shame rise to the surface. I don't feel connected to anyone or anything; I don't understand how to live and I don't know how to speak. My voice is so small, so quiet, and she can't coerce it out of me, no matter what she says.

I continue to listen to her in silence as she sits at her glass dressing table. I wait for her to leave, seeing her walk down the corridor to watch a television show with my father then sit down on the red puffy stool where I can see my face from all sides in the mirror. It's a place where I have spent ages looking at myself, wondering what I look like; seeing my nose one side and then the other. I listen carefully to make sure the TV is on and my parents are settled, and feel a rush at the thought of doing something that I'm not allowed to do.

I pull open the dressing-table drawer to find buttons and loose thread, some jewellery and lots of pieces of paper all folded up. I open them carefully. Mostly I'm looking at receipts, some from years ago. I don't understand why she keeps them. Some are newspaper clippings from the

Jewish Chronicle, revealing the death of a family member, a wedding, or a birth, the paper now yellow and dry. I wonder if she remembers keeping them.

I think I hear the door leading to the hallway open so I start to quickly put everything back exactly how it was and hide behind the door until I realise it's just my imagination. My heart is racing as I think about her finding me.

'Zara, what are you doing, looking through my things?' I imagine her asking.

I would respond: 'I'm not looking for anything in particular. I just want to know if you have any secrets that you haven't told me.'

She would say back to me: 'What exactly are you looking for?'

I would answer as honestly as I could: 'I'm just looking for something, Mum. I don't really know what, but I will know when I find it, and when I find it, I will tell you.'

And my mother would look at me with her blue eyes, a little confused by my behaviour, as she was most days, and say gently, 'I would rather you didn't look in my drawers, they're private.'

If I could have been really honest, I would have told her the truth: 'But you don't understand, Mum. I can't stop, I do this all the time – I don't know why, I just feel the need to keep looking. And I don't even know what I'm looking for.'

But we never did have that conversation. No one ever

caught me, and nothing new was ever put in that drawer. It wasn't until her death that I realised I'd been looking in the wrong place. All those years of going through her things I had never made the connection of what I wanted to find. Everything I wanted to know was in the old brown leathery suitcase, tucked high up in the cupboard above her dressing table, pushed to the back, where I would find information on my adoption and letters, the saddest one of all from my mother writing to the adoption agency, asking them for a baby.

Dear Sir,

My Husband and I are professional people; we could give a baby a lovely home.

I have always read a lot of books and I would make sure this baby had all the education that it needed. I have wanted to become a Mother from when I was very young but sadly due to medical issues this will not happen for me.

I have had miscarriages and have been told that I will never be able to carry a baby to full term. My husband will do anything to make me happy. He is a judge, and would like to be a Father too.

I had never imagined this would happen to me and I cannot imagine a life without children. I am very good with children and have baby-sat from a very young age.

I am now thirty-three; I know I am older now as a woman to become a mother, but I am in good health. Please would you kindly consider me as an adoptive parent?

You can come over and look at our house, it's very nice.

I will wait to hear from you.

Thank you for considering me.

* * *

I have very few memories of myself as a young girl. What I do remember quite clearly are the feelings, the fear, the clinging onto my mother's hand in strange places. The way she walked so fast down the street that I could barely keep up with her. My heart bouncing and pounding in my chest if I was ever made to walk into a room with strangers and say hello.

'Zara, run over and play with that little girl.' My mum's gentle but stern voice would say. But it only made me cling to her harder.

'Zara, you walk inside first. You're a big girl, you can do it.'

I knew my mother loved me but I also saw her irritation with me for being the way I was as a child: I was too shut down, too quiet, too sad. She could never understand why I was the way I was, and I could never explain.

And next came the broken-hearted memories. When for

what felt like the millionth time my mother had to pick me up in the night from a friend's house because of the panic and separation that I felt each time I was left apart from her. Or the time I went to Spain with my friend's family and cried every single day, feeling such dread and fear that something was going to happen to my mother. Sometimes I still feel the embarrassment and humiliation within myself just thinking about it – I just couldn't seem to do what other little girls so easily could.

'I just don't understand you, Zara. This is getting ridiculous. You need to stay away from home for one night, you're not a baby,' she said to me as I felt the instant relief of walking back into our house.

'When are you going to stay away one night?' she asked again, looking me in the eye sternly as I felt the panic rise. When she was angry I couldn't speak. I was only nine or ten, but I felt shame seeping into every part of my body.

'What a baby!' my brother Gary chimed in. 'Do you know how silly this is? How old are you, three?'

My mother did nothing to stop him that evening. I remember her drained-looking face in the kitchen and I knew that she had already grown tired of me, I was wearing her down.

I had stood quietly between my mother and my brother, unable to stop the hot tears falling down my cheeks at the shocking realisation that my own family could turn from me when I needed their comfort most. That's when the longing really started, the dreaming of my birth mother. Some days she was as kind as my adopted mother could be, other days, just as cold.

* * *

I pick up the phone as I lay on the floor of my friend's flat, curled up in a ball, foetal-like. I am a couple of months drug-free.

'James, I can't do this. It's too hard.' I hear the self-pity in my voice.

'Sweetie,' he says gently. 'It's okay, just for today, that's all. Come to the lunchtime meeting, we'll be there.'

'I keep dreaming about things, it's too much.'

'Zara, God will protect you. You're ready to feel it all now. Feelings don't kill us. You know that, right?'

'God is always your answer. I'm finding this all a bit too religious for me.' I can hear James trying not to laugh. 'I don't know who I believe in, James, but I need the dreams to stop. How do I make that happen?' I ask wearily.

'You just need to trust, sweetie, and let them surface. This is the stuff you've been running from. I think it needs to come out, you have to trust,' he repeats.

'Trust, trust, trust… Is that your answer to everything?'

He lets out a thick laugh. 'Yes,' he says. 'Just try it. Don't give up before the miracle.'

Somebody's Daughter

Feeling myself smile at these trite words, I lie back, wrap myself in a soft blanket and let the dreams come.

3

North London, 1981

I hear a hammering on my bedroom door, revealing the growing desperation within my brother. We were late teens now. I hadn't been home long from a late-night party. Sitting up in the early morning light, I can see my door opening and the shadow of my brother appear.

'What?' I half-whisper, 'what do you want?'

'I need cigarettes, you selfish slut! Where are they?'

I point towards my bag and he pounces on it, rifles through, his almost bare butt facing me. But I don't grumble as he tosses my stuff around – I had finally learned in the last few months that it was wise to be quiet when he was like this, needing his drug. Cigarettes only dulled the craving for a few moments. I'd let him smoke the whole pack; as long as he didn't touch me, I didn't care.

Somebody's Daughter

My brother Gary was two and a half years older than me and also adopted. I knew he had struggled since he was young to cope with it from the way he would say in anger to our Mother: 'You're not my real mother!' After these outbursts they would have long conversations locked in his room. I was never allowed in, it was private. Sometimes I would go and lie on my floor and try and listen through the vents to see if I could hear what they talked about. He had started stealing at a young age and I understood that need to steal. I felt 'stolen' too, just the way I think he did. For how do we know that we weren't stolen away from our natural mothers? I had always worried about him, checking to see if he was still breathing, still alive after taking so many drugs, but my concern was turning to hatred.

'I'm so glad we're not really related. Your mother must have been the biggest whore in England. That's why she didn't want you, whore baby!' he snarled as he left the room. The words barely stung, I was so used to them. He was by now a full-blown heroin addict. I don't know who took the drug first but it seemed that a few of his friends were all taking it. They would all come to our house and sit in his bedroom, the burnt tin foil covering his floor. He had only taken a few hits for the drug to get a hold on him, a tight grip that now controlled him. But he didn't believe that. I had learned that the hard way, thinking that pointing it out would make him stop. It never worked, of course, but what did I know at sixteen? His anger exacerbated the more out-of-control he became. A public schoolboy heroin addict who bullied everyone around him, I was his main target. I soon learned the best way to dodge a bullet was to be one step ahead and quick on my feet so as not to get too bruised. I would sneak past his door and stay away from him as much as I could.

* * *

I'm almost asleep again when Adam, my brother's school friend, comes creeping in. He often sleeps over on the weekends and I've had a crush on him since I was twelve. None of my brother's friends has ever shown an interest in me – I'm just the cute baby sister – until last week when Adam and I found ourselves alone at a party after his girlfriend left. We were sitting on the sofa, both a little stoned, when he leaned over and we started kissing.

Adam stands by my bed. I can see his tall, slender outline.

'What are you doing?' I whisper.

Silently, he slides into the bed next to me and I begin to giggle.

'*Shhh…*' he murmurs. 'You'll wake up the whole house.'

'You have a girlfriend,' I say sternly.

'Oh, but I like you, you know that. I've seen the way you look at me, I know you like me too. I really liked that kiss the other night.'

'I'm way too young for you. You boys always tell me I'm just the little sister,' I whisper back, feeling his body pressing against me.

'But the little sister is growing up. You're very sexy, did you know that?' he says softly, sliding his hands under my T-shirt to brush against my breasts.

I feel a little afraid as he kisses me gently before quickly forcing his tongue in my mouth. Then I kiss him back. It was true I had a crush on him, but he is four years older than me – I'm not sure I'm ready for this.

He tugs on my underwear, his hands between my legs, and all I can think is how quickly he got to second base. My body responds in spite of my fear: it feels good, exciting. He won't stop kissing me. *He really wants me*, I think. Then, without realising what he's doing, I feel a searing pain. He pushes so hard, I cry out and he has to put his hands over my mouth to quieten me.

Did this mean he would give up his girlfriend and now be my boyfriend? It must. But why does it hurt so much? No one had told me it would be like this.

He pushes inside me again for a moment, the pain making me scream into his hands, my body trembling from all the confusing sensations. After holding me for a few moments, he clumsily gets up.

'I need to get out your room before everyone wakes up,' he mutters.

I lie frozen in the bed, not sure how I had allowed this to happen – I had thought we would just keep kissing. But I didn't think this was actual sex. I'm dizzy, confused and slightly exhilarated. I know I can never tell any of my friends the truth of what happened – they would think I had given myself away too easily.

Adam did not become my boyfriend, although he smiled at me the next morning. A week later, he crept back into my room. I wasn't sure how, but I had become his secret. Just like all those years before, I couldn't seem to find the voice to make it stop.

* * *

I knew that to knock on my brother's door was suicide but sometimes I was lonely and even though I didn't mind my own company a part of me really believed I could make friends with him. Then maybe he would be nicer to me and living in this house would be more bearable.

'What do you want, slut?'

He is sitting up on his bed, thick cigarette smoke filling the room. Blackened tinfoil is scattered all over the floor. He has just taken a hit, so his mood is calm – he's always much better like this.

I perch tentatively on the edge of the bed.

'Do you have any weed?'

He laughs. 'Oh, Zara's a little pothead now! Yeah, sure –

little sixteen-year-old pothead.' Coughing and spluttering, he rolls a joint and turns on the TV. We sit and watch a show, nothing I'm interested in, and for one small moment I feel his acceptance.

A few moments later, Adam shows up. I feel my insides shake with excitement.

'Hey, Zara.'

I smile back, but as I shift on the bed to make room for him to sit, I momentarily block my brother's view of the TV. Without warning, I feel a violent kick to my head. My skull slams into the wall.

'Move out the fucking way, you stupid bitch!' he yells.

'Easy, Gary,' is all Adam can say.

I stay for a moment, fighting the tears. All I can think about is the humiliation of Adam seeing me this way. My head is screaming at me to get up and walk out, but it takes another ten minutes for me to do so. As I open Gary's door I meet my mother in the corridor, with her usual bubbly smile. I smile back at her and then as soon as she's gone, I run into my bedroom and lie on my bed, pulling the blankets over me.

* * *

My brother is giving me a ride to work. I'm a waitress. I don't know what else to do now that I'm out of school and he works behind the bar so it seemed to make sense. Mum thinks it's safe for him to take me to work, but there's always a detour on the way home.

'I won't be a moment,' says Gary, pulling up the car behind a mass of identical concrete flats.

'What number will you be in?' I ask.

'I'm not telling you. Stay here and wait.' He gets out of the car, his jeans loose around his waist.

'Please don't be long. You always say you'll just be a few minutes,' I yell out of the door. 'I'm tired, I want to go home.'

'I'm just picking something up. You wanted a lift, didn't you?' he snarls back at me. 'Stay in the car, you selfish little bitch, and wait.'

So I sit and wait, looking towards the flats every few moments, hoping he'll come out any minute. I'm tired, thirsty, and getting angry.

Why do I fall for this every time? He wasn't going to come out quickly, he was going to sit and use with his dealer. Why did I always expect him to do something different? He was always so good at convincing me. I shift in my seat. He has taken the keys. I don't know where I am; there's no payphone, and who would I call anyway? An hour drags by slowly.

What if he doesn't come back? What if he's dead? What if he's left me here for the whole night?

I feel my anger rising, a rage that is getting harder to suppress. Why am I such an idiot? I hate myself for my stupidity; I hate him more and more every day. Another hour goes by with no sign of him. Would my mother be worried, I wonder. No, she thought I was safe with my brother. What a joke that was.

Opening the car door, I walk up to one of the buildings, but hearing voices and a door slam, I run back to the car. I'm afraid of what he would do if he caught me snooping. Sitting back in the car, my heart racing, I try to sleep. And then he's back, opening the car door aggressively and swaying slightly; his eyes are red. I start shouting, a big mistake. 'Where were you? You left me here for two hours! How could you do that to me? I know you were using again. I'm sick of you…'

He grabs me harshly and flings me against the seat, spitting in my face.

'Shut up, you fucking bitch.'

My eyes are burning with tears. I want to get away from him, but I don't know how it's ever going to be possible.

'Dinner's ready.' My mother smiles as we walk into the house. 'You both hungry?' She is prodding potatoes with a fork. I look at her and almost speak, but what would be the point? She won't listen, especially when it comes to my brother. She can't see it, or doesn't want to; it scares her too much. One problem child is already enough. As for my father, he doesn't even know us. He rarely even talks to us – he's blind to everything that doesn't involve being given dinner and a cup of tea.

* * *

I make it to the lunchtime meeting, squeezing into a seat between the 'boys' as I like to call them. I'm beginning to enjoy the meetings. This feeling I have inside of me, it's something new, something I've never felt before. I think it might be hope, or at least a sense of being understood. The grip of needing the drugs is loosening. I realise that a whole week has gone past with no cravings. My thirst has become stronger, but it's a thirst through relief at staying sober: I was doing it. My emotions, though still in charge, were being diffused as I talked. I was aware that I was feeling things at a new level as I hung onto every word I heard in the meetings; they were right. As corny as it sounds, their message was working.

'Feelings are not facts.'

'First things first.'

'One day at a time.'

The slogans were printed around the room in every meeting.

I still had trouble identifying with the old men who had drunk away their lives, but I identified with some of the younger people, with the inability to cope with their feelings, the depression, the constant insecurity. Wide awake now, it felt so good: I walked looking at the trees and the sky without being buried inside my own mind; I noticed life in a new way.

What was now surfacing and harder to push away was the

longing, the hunger I'd had before I picked up that drug to bury it. I needed to know my truth; I wanted to understand why my birth mother gave me away. Was I an ugly baby? How could she have walked away from me? What was my story? I couldn't live my life on Chapter Two anymore. To move forward, I needed my Chapter One. I haven't yet shared this directly with anyone; instead I make the same jokes to my newfound sober friends that I had made all my life.

'She probably won't remember, she might not even care. What if she has her own life now? I don't want to hurt anyone. What if she's royalty? What if she's a whore? Maybe I'm the product of rape? What if she says she doesn't want to know? I can't hurt my adoptive parents, my mother would be devastated.'

'Have you ever thought, Zara that she might have spent her whole life thinking about you? Maybe you finding her will heal her,' Terry tells me at lunch.

'She gave me up,' I reply sternly. 'What kind of mother gives up her baby?'

'A woman that has no support. It's just a thought, Zara. You don't know the truth because no one has told you, but maybe it's time to find out.'

James has remained silent all this time.

'You're not very talkative for a talkative person,' I tell him. I'm trying to be funny.

'I'm a birth father,' he replies quietly.

I feel my body tighten, part of me not wanting to hear this.

'I had a little girl, but her mother was an addict and I was drinking. I ended up in prison, so they took her away,' he adds.

I can see the pain etched on his face. I had never met a birth parent before and I didn't know how to respond.

'It was the right thing, Zara.' I'm shaking my head. 'I couldn't take care of her. I was in prison, her mother was a junkie and she needed a family to care of her.'

'But you're sober now, you have been for years. It's not right, James, you're her father and she needs to know who you are.' My eyes are filling with tears. I feel a sudden distance from James, whom I had grown so fond of. Why hadn't he told me this before? 'You need to find her.'

'It will happen in time, when she's ready.'

At this I'm angry – no, furious. I can't hide it. 'Do you think about her?'

'Not a day goes past when I don't.' He pulls up his sleeve to reveal a tattoo: it says 'Annie Rose'.

'But she doesn't know you're thinking about her. You need to tell her, you need to find her!' I'm aware that I'm yelling now.

Later, I lie in bed, unable to sleep. I think about James, his daughter, Annie Rose, and why he's in my life: a man who has given up his child is helping to save my life. I know there's some deep meaning in this, but I can't even begin to know what it might be.

4

London, 1982

'Happy birthday to you, happy birthday to you…' my mother sings in her shrill voice. I smile, looking at my birthday cake and its seventeen candles. She smiles back, her eyes shiny with tears. I'm high again, but she doesn't seem to notice. Or if she does, she doesn't say anything. I'm exhausted, having had sex with my boyfriend for most of the night. The lines of speed I've taken are still in my system, the slow crash beginning to bring my mood back. Closing my eyes to blow out the candles, I see images of his hands caressing my body, between my legs, tying me to his bed, and then the thumping on the door, his wife screaming.

'I thought you were separated,' I wail as he runs to the door, wrapping a sheet around his naked body.

Somebody's Daughter

'We are, I just need to calm her down.'

He trips on the sheet.

'Can you untie me first?'

He doesn't respond.

'Oh great!' I wiggle my hands a little, trying to get one out from the knot hold binding my wrists, which are now starting to burn. A torrent of Italian is going back and forth between them. I don't need to understand the words, it's easy to hear the rage. My lover might have been taken to be a true native. He is so fluent and enamoured by everything Italian; he even looks somewhat Italian himself, dark hair covering his whole body.

Fiorella, his estranged wife, walks into the bedroom, black hair falling over her face. She looks at me tied to the bed, my body bare for all to see.

'You English whore! You English bitch!' she screams with venom.

'I'm sorry,' I say as politely as I can. 'He told me you were no longer together, and you don't live together. I thought it was okay.' Wriggling some more, one hand finally comes free enough for me to pull a bed sheet over myself.

'You are so young, he is still my husband,' she spits disgustedly as she leaves the room.

George leaves with her, speaking calmly, pleadingly, to her. He does not return for another two hours. I stay in the room, jealous now of this woman who he has claimed is no longer his. I lie in his bed, flicking through the channels on TV and manage to reach over to the ashtray to smoke a joint that I find there. I should leave, I tell myself; anyone with any sense of decency would. He deserves to be left, but I don't go – I can't. I'm pathetic and I know it.

George wanders back in a few hours later, a sultry smile on his face.

'You did look pretty tied up like that.'

I half-smile as he slides into bed beside me.

'Do you know you're the first woman I've been with who wasn't Italian?'

'I don't know what I am,' I whisper as he starts kissing me again.

'Well, whatever you are, I want some more of it. Now, where were we…?'

'Zara, Zara! You're in a daze.' My mother is still smiling. 'Blow out the candles. Do you not like the cake? It's chocolate – you're never too old for chocolate cake.'

'I love chocolate cake, you know that. Thanks, Mum.'

I see the look of concern on her face, yet she doesn't say a word; she just holds my gaze for a moment until I look away. I take a big bite of cake and make all the right noises of satisfaction until I see her relax.

* * *

As I sit in the meetings alongside my new sober friends, I'm aware that there are so many shameful things about my past that I'm not yet ready to tell them. I'd not only used drugs to escape my feelings about myself and my family, but I'd also used sex: I was addicted to the false sense of intimacy I felt when I was high and with a new guy. I loved the game, the chase, the way a man pursued me. But afterwards I felt differently. All the power and self-esteem I felt in those fleeting moments melted away. Once the act was done, I felt like the skin shed by a snake. Those feelings made me want to get high all over again. Now I began to see the connection: I knew I needed some time alone.

I'm trying to stay away from a married man that I have worked for, a man called Simon. He's been trying to contact me about a supposed job. He wants me back in his bed and the urge to go to him is still just as strong. I know he can't offer me anymore than sex, that it will still be the same as all the other emotionless meetings I've had with men. I know that my life depends on me making good choices for myself.

So I say no to the job, that I'm busy. I can feel the fear as I place the receiver down. I've spent the last two years touring with pop bands as a backing vocalist, spending weeks away on the road, and performing on TV shows. I loved to perform and sing, and I enjoyed the lifestyle but had to admit that it wasn't the best environment for me; it was so easy to act out sexually and continue my drug use. I have hardly any money in my account, but I know I need to try and do as James has suggested, trust that things will work themselves out and only take the work that I can handle without me trying to control everything. I'm twenty-three years old; it's time to try doing things differently.

Then I make another phone call. I had looked up the number a few weeks ago. It's now staring at me from a piece of paper on the floor. I dial the number for the National Adoption Society. I'm twenty-three years of age. I can't lie anymore about my need to know, now that I'm living drug–free; I can no longer hide the truth and pretend that I don't care. I need to know, I've always needed to know. No matter how my adopted parents might feel, I have to find out my story and why she gave me up. I've been given the number for the director of social workers, from whom I can request information regarding my adoption.

I'm living in a small room in East Finchley, North London. I have my bed, a fridge and the shower all in one room. There's a shared toilet in the hallway. It's my first time living alone and I'm grateful for the solitude. I'm working a little bit here and there, doing some gigs with some well-known bands and writing and performing with some of the sober guys in AA. Cleaning houses, babysitting, signing on and off the dole. I need the time to focus on myself without rushing away for long periods.

Somebody's Daughter

I find myself hoovering whenever I see one little bit of dirt on the floor.

'Zara,' Terry says. 'You're addicted to your Hoover, maybe you need to join a new support group?"

I'm staying clean; I'm keeping away from my old relationships. I have started my search.

It turns out the appointment with the social worker is in the same borough that I live in now. I arrive at reception to find that Jane, my flatmate from a couple of years ago, is now working there. It's a shock to have such a reminder of my old life and I wonder if the universe is trying to tell me something. Already I'm nervous, filled with guilt and a deep sense of betrayal towards my adoptive parents.

'I knew it was you. It had to be.' She smiles. 'Are you here to find her…?' Her voice trails off.

'Yes. Well, I think so. I'm going to make a start.' She smiles back at me. 'But please don't say anything to anyone.'

She is reassuring, at least. I sit looking at her, thinking about the chaos we caused, three girls living together in our first time away from home; the amount of drugs consumed in that place. I had had to stay away from them all. We used to be so close, so knitted together in that way of life. A few months of staying clean was not a lot, I knew, but it was enough to allow me a glimpse back: it was not where I wanted to be anymore.

'Zara, you can go up now,' Jane calls to me cheerily.

'Good luck, let me know what happens.' I nod back at her and make my way up in the lift.

The room is small and chilly. The social worker is shorter than me, with thick dark hair. She seems warm and kind though and I'm immediately relaxed.

'So,' she says, 'I have all your forms filled out. Adopted people are now allowed to access the information you need to find your birth families, since the law changed in 1975. I do, however, suggest that you get some emotional support. Counselling is available. There can be many expectations during a reunion. Do you have any support?'

'Oh yes, I'm sober and in the 12-step Program. I have lots of support. I'm in a great place these days.' I'm bluffing, worried that if I don't present myself confidently she may withhold some information that is rightfully mine. I know I'm convincing – I've always been good at hiding what's really going on inside, I'm still a performer.

'Well, if you're sure you don't need our services,' she responds.

'I don't,' I respond quickly. 'But thank you.'

'Okay, my dear. Here are your papers. I'm not supposed to give all of these to you, but if I were you, I'd want to know everything I could. I managed to photocopy most of your file. Please don't tell my office.' She laughs.

My bravado is fading, my heart beating harder. I sit up straight in my chair, unable to speak. I've spent so long knowing and longing, but now it's finally here I'm not sure I'm ready for the next step.

Before I can stop it all, she hands me the papers, but before she lets go of them she says, 'Your mother's name is Patricia Sampson.' Just like that. *Your mother's name is Patricia Sampson.* Her words echo in my head. She looks at me for a response but I've been caught off guard. My head is swimming. She had access to my mother's name? All these years of not knowing, and this woman has my information just like that? Was it that easy? I feel a sudden surge of anger.

'I know, dear…' She says 'dear' just like my adopted mother does, which irritates me no end. 'It's a lot to take in.'

'So, she is real then,' I hear myself saying. 'She's a real person, this isn't just a dream. I really am adopted.'

She is looking at me, confused by my comment.

'Yes, she's a real person. I think you should take the forms home and spend some time looking over them. We can meet again next week and decide how you would like to proceed.'

I nod.

'I suggest you order your birth certificate, dear. You might get some information on your birth father and more on your mother.'

I don't like that she's calling this woman my mother – I already have a mother.

'And your name was…' She shuffles through the papers.

'Paula, Paula Sampson. That's the name on your original birth certificate.'

'She named me?' I'm half-whispering. 'She named me? She cared enough to name me? I always thought I was just a number.'

As I walk home, my mind contains only one thought repeating over and over, Patricia Sampson: she has a name, she exists. As soon as I walk through my front door I lie down on the floor, scattering the papers around my feet and start to read.

Application Inquiry.
MOTHER and BABY
Age 17. Jewish. Shorthand typist. Smart, attractive little girl.
HAIR. Mass of black hair just like the Chinese!
Colouring. Darkish.
EYES. Deep blue.
Baby rather cute of her type, mother says she's the image of her mother at that age.
PUTATIVE FATHER.
Name Antonio. Hair, Brown. Eyes, Brown.
AGE. 22
ITALIAN.
Met him at a club.

Somebody's Daughter

I sit up and reread the paper again: Italian. I'm half-Italian? I do have a father after all. He exists too. My mind is calm as I stare at the wall. Maybe an hour goes by, I'm not sure.

I glance at the other papers, my tears beginning to fall, catching the pages with a splash. I suppose that's appropriate, who knows what you're supposed to do in this situation? There are letters too – written to my birth mother about how I'm doing, how much weight I've gained, how much I eat, how much my adopted parents love me.

I can't stop the tears from coming now: the harder I cry, the more sound erupts from within me. I can hear a long howl and I can't seem to stop it – it's like the lid has been taken off. I'm forever changed. I now know some of my story. As I cry, the feeling of pain is familiar, almost a comfort in a strange way: for the first time in my life I'm allowing myself to grieve the loss of my parents. Time stands still as the day turns into night and I sleep, restful, surrounded by the pages of my life. The next day I wake early and head back to the council building to order my birth certificate, filling out my name as Paula Sampson; I realise it's the first time I've ever written it down. I sit on the hard-backed wooden chair and smoke two cigarettes, one after the other. It takes me a moment to get up after I'm called as I don't recognise the name that the lady is calling.

She hands me a sheet of folded pink paper and I open it, scanning every word. There's my mother's address. I look for my father's full name, but he's not mentioned on the certificate at all. I'm disappointed, I can't help but be – it's like putting a jigsaw together and realising you're missing the final piece.

I spend the rest of the day unfolding and rereading the pink paper, unable to put it down. It's like I've finally been awakened and I have a new purpose.

I know the area where my mother once lived and a couple of days later I drive with a friend to the very building. It's a block of brick flats on Gunnersbury Avenue, West London. She pulls over and we sit quietly for a moment.

'Ready?' she asks.

I nod.

My heart pounds as I open the car door. A light rain is beginning to fall against the grey sky so we hurry inside and creep up the stairs until we're standing outside their door. There's post sticking out from the letterbox.

'Look at the mail,' my friend whispers.

I'm certain my breathing is so loud it can be heard inside. I listen at the door but there's no sound. I gently lift the letterbox, sliding out an envelope to see the name: it's not theirs. I shake my head and we tiptoe back down the stairs with some relief, running back across the street to the safety of the car.

'They don't live there anymore, there are different surnames on the post,' I say, panting, as I get my breath back. But my heart won't stop racing – my mother lived in that very building once, when she was pregnant with me. There's a park opposite and I can't help but wonder if she walked through it while I was inside her.

* * *

My days change so much. No longer travelling or doing as many gigs, I'm now cleaning a house, claiming benefits, going to meetings and spending a lot of time at Catherine House. Catherine House is the place where people go to get their birth, death and marriage certificates. I'd not been there before but I loved the place from the moment I walked into the old building. Huge rooms with file upon file, hundreds of them, holding endless names between their pages, going back years. I enjoy the anonymity of the place.

Where do I even begin? I have my birth mother's maiden name, now I need to find out if she got married. Then I'll look to see if she has had children. I feel confident and focused; I have a plan.

I find the letters I need and pull down a large volume, opening the file on the wooden desk. The print is so tiny; there are so many names. I slowly start my way down, reading name after name. It takes me a long time but at last I see her, my mother. Yes, she did indeed get married. She now has a different surname and it's Italian. I double-check the information before I write it down.

Italian… Did she marry my birth father?

I go to the front desk and fill out the long form that will allow me to see her marriage certificate. It seems crazy that just anyone is allowed to get this information but I'm grateful for it all the same and eager to learn as much as I can.

I don't want it getting lost in the post, so I return three days later to collect it. I find a space in the corner and open the paper: I have another address, this time in Kensington. Now I can look to see if they had any children. I also decide to track her mother's name, my grandmother, just to make sure I have the correct family. But there's a spelling mistake on her maiden name – the one I have from my file doesn't match the one I found in the index.

I must be looking confused, because a man amidst the rows of files and papers walks up to me.

'You look lost,' he says kindly.

'Does it show?' I reply.

He laughs, and hands me his card.

'I'm a searcher – I help adopted people find one another and any family members that are missing.'

'I'm adopted,' I say. 'I have my mother's name.'

'Well, then you're way ahead of many people. You can do this yourself.'

'I have a problem, though – I have two spellings of my grandmother's last name, I could easily go on the wrong track.'

'What does your intuition say?' he asks.

I stare back down at the book and the paper I'm holding. 'This one,' I point. 'I'm sure this is her.'

'Then you're most probably right. So much of a search is about listening to your intuition.' And with that, he wishes me luck before fading back into the shelves.

I look again, checking the feeling inside myself. By the end of the day I have ordered more certificates for my birth mother, including her youngest child.

I'm in a daze most of the time now, present but not really; the search is consuming me. I'm beginning to dream more, aware that the shadow of my birth mother that I always felt beside me is now slowly coming into view.

I visit my mum and dad and avoid all questions. I'm faltering between a feeling of such terrible betrayal towards them, and a newfound strength. It has nothing to do with them, however strange that may sound considering they adopted me and probably know information about my birth mother: they sent her all those letters, letters I've seen. But this is about my need now. How am I supposed to explain that to them? I've hated myself for so long, but more so now that I'm sober I see how important it is to stop those negative voices in my head.

I dream vividly each night. I'm always looking for something, searching desperately. I go into our house, the house I grew up in and that my parents still live in, but in my dreams it's been abandoned, every room full of cobwebs; dust covers the furniture, sheets cover the sofas. Into each room I walk purposefully, opening every door, steady in my search. Often I find myself walking into my parents' bedroom, where I stand on a chair to reach the highest cupboard in the room and take down the many cardboard boxes stacked there. There are endless boxes stacked on top of each other. Finally, right at the back of the cupboard, is a tiny shoebox. I stretch to reach it, stepping down from the chair as I carefully remove the lid. I jump back: inside is a tiny, crying baby so ugly it almost looks like a monster. I take the child out, holding it tightly until it is soothed, and then I wake up.

* * *

I have my birth mother's address from her youngest child's birth certificate. It's not far from where I'm living. But I can't bring myself to call, scared somehow my voice will be recognised, however mad that sounds, so I get my friend to call the neighbours to check my information is up-to-date. A girl answers and says that she knew them and that they'd been neighbours for years. She says on the phone that she knows Pat (my mother) and her son and daughter – that's how I found out I had a sister as when I was searching at Catherine House, I didn't find her, only my brother. My friend tells her that her mother was an old friend of her mother's. She says they moved out of London. She doesn't know where, but if my friend were to call back on Saturday night, her mother would be at her house as they're having a party and she would know where they went.

My friend is going away and can't help me so she urges me to do it instead.

'Zara, they won't recognise your voice. Just call. We have a story, remember? Say she's a friend of your mother's. I doubt they'll even ask.'

My palms are sweating as Saturday comes around. As I dial the number my heart beats rapidly. I can hear music in the background as the girl answers.

'Er, hello? I'm the girl that called the other day about the Giocondis. Is your mother there?'

'Oh yes,' she says brightly, 'hang on a mo.'

Their house must be full of people, I think, as I hear passing conversations. I wait for what feels like an eternity and then the phone clicks.

'Me mum says they moved to Weybridge.'

And that's it. A quick goodbye from the stranger and my search is over: I have found her.

5

North London, 1988

My mum – my adoptive mum, that is – is ill a lot. I don't ever remember a time when she wasn't struggling with some illness. She had open-heart surgery not long ago, when she was just fifty. I worry about her health and she knows that I do, but I find her as hard to be around as she finds me: we irritate one another. There is no acceptance from either side; I try, but always seem to fail within minutes. Every word that comes from my mouth she takes the wrong way, and every word that she says to me I take as a criticism. As time has gone by, I feel that we are on a constant treadmill and I wonder when or if we'll ever get off.

In spite of it all, I still go and visit. Pulling the car into the driveway, I think about a particularly terrible fight where my anger was just pouring out of me, my pain raw with no control, and she faked a heart attack right in front of my eyes. She fell to the floor, clutching her chest. I stood glued to the spot, unable to move. The rage that I felt turned to a panic at the thought of losing her.

'You're killing me,' she had said. 'You're killing me.' For once, my brother came to my aid. He walked into the room to see her lying on my bedroom floor and me screaming hysterically that she was dead. 'Oh, for God's sake, woman, get up,' he told her in a booming voice – and she did. She got up, straightened her Margaret Thatcher-style dress, wiped her make-up and went down to open the front door to the builder, who had apparently been knocking this whole time, as if nothing had happened at all.

Today, I unlock the front door, calling out to her that I'm here. My father is watching television and my mother is in the kitchen. She seems happy to see me. She hugs me warmly, her huge bosoms comforting against me, in spite of everything. I need her still to love me: she is my anchor and she knows it.

I listen to my mother talk and I wish I could tell her what I'm doing, that I have found the woman who gave birth to me. I want to tell her that without this woman she could never have had me. But I protect her, because I know her pain about not being able to have children. It has been revealed in certain moments and I don't want to inflict more.

If I could have told my mother the truth as a little girl, when she was frustrated with my silence, if she were truly able to listen, I would have said just three simple words:

'I want my mother.'

But she was my mother, so she wouldn't have understood what I meant and what good would it have done? As far as she has always been concerned I had her, I had my mother. I can't hate her for that. But now that I'm so close to finding my biological mother, I realise that it's always been a fantasy: there is no real mother for me anymore, I don't fully belong to either of them.

I'm trying to be a better, less selfish daughter. I tell my mum that I'm going to meetings. She has little to say about it, but I sense she approves.

My brother is back living at home and we're civil to each other. I'm less scared of him now, but I don't go out of my way to talk to him. No longer sober, he has relapsed. I'm saddened, as he did so well for a while but I know that I can't save him anymore. When I visit, I try to be kind and I leave as soon as I feel irritated again.

'I managed to stay a whole half an hour without losing it,' I tell James proudly when we meet up later that day. He laughs heartily. 'Well done, girl, well done!'

* * *

Somebody's Daughter

I'm in my car, driving with my friend Kate to spy on my birth mother. The windows are down; the sky looks like honey today. I have her address. Once I knew the area where they had moved to from the old neighbour I called Directory Enquiries and got her number and address. I called the number to make sure that it worked, my hands trembling. My girlfriend was watching me.

A woman's voice answers. 'Hello, hello?" she says into the silence. After a lingering moment I put the phone down. I know that she owns an Italian restaurant with her husband, that they have two children, and that she lives in a normal house in a normal neighbourhood. I feel relieved.

I realise her husband is unlikely to be my birth father.

'So obviously she has a thing for Italians.' I'm laughing with my friend. 'And I can't say I blame her – I just hope my father isn't some fat ugly one wearing a medallion. Now that would be depressing.'

We find the street and start counting the numbers. I can feel the fear invade my insides.

'It's this one.'

I slow down. It's a nice detached house with a sports car in the driveway. I park on the kerb opposite, half-hidden by some trees, and get my lunch out of my bag.

'You brought lunch?' Kate is stunned. 'How can you possibly eat?'

'Er, because I'm hungry.'

We wait in silence, looking at the house, but I'm not really sure what I'm waiting for. I take another bite of my sandwich.

'Do you want to see her?' Kate asks.

'No, I don't think I do. I want to leave.' I stuff the sandwich back in the bag.

'Just wait a few more moments,' she whispers.

Their front door opens and instinctively I sink down in my seat. A man walks to the end of the driveway and calls out a name. For a moment he looks directly at our car.

I start the engine and drive away.

* * *

I decide I can't just land on my mother like that, I have to write to her first – but what am I supposed to say? So I visit my social worker, Ms Cameron, who offers to help. I agonise over every word of my letter.

'What if her husband has no idea about me and she opens it in front of him? What if she forgets that she had a baby…?' My voice trails off.

'No woman,' she says gently, 'ever forgets she had a baby.'

'Are you sure?' I ask.

'Yes, dear, I'm sure.'

Dear Mrs Giocondi,
I am trying on behalf of my client to trace members of

a family to whom she believes she may be connected.

The name of the family she wishes to trace is Sampson and they lived in the Ealing area around 1964.

If you feel you can help and would like to discuss this further then contact me either by letter, or by telephone at the above number.

In all cases where one is trying to trace members of families who have lost touch, it is common to write to people who have no connection with the people involved and if this is so, I am sorry to have troubled you.

Yours sincerely,
Ms Cameron

As much as it hasn't come from me, I still decide that I want to be the one to post the letter, in my own time. Sick to my stomach, I walk absentmindedly in the near darkness back from her office to my little one-room bedsit. I'm clutching the letter too tightly, my hand aching from the pressure.

Do I post it now and get it over with?

I feel panicky, intense butterflies that I have never felt before fill my stomach, almost jumping out of my throat. The wave of nausea passes.

I could hold onto the letter another day and give myself more time, I think for a moment, but even though I wish I could,

I know that Pandora's Box has already been cracked open. In life some people can turn a blind eye, pretend they don't want the things they want because it's safer. But I was never that type of person. The voice in my head speaks loudly, interrupting the endless thoughts.

Zara, it's time.

I can see the red gleam of the post box in the distance. I'm afraid, but what am I afraid of? Rejection. That she won't want to know me. Of hurting my adopted mother. Of knowing the truth of how I came into existence.

I place the envelope at the mouth of the post box and let myself linger. I pull it away for one second, an inch from the opening. Then I inhale and let go. And with that, I have no idea what else to do with myself, so I decide to head for a meeting to see if anyone I know is there. My mind is racing and I need a bit of grounding to keep me focused. I'm drawn to the passing faces as my car comes to a standstill.

I'm almost hoping I might see the face of my most recent ex, Simon – he often walks this way. I try to avert my mind from him but it keeps pulling me back. My ex-lover, a man who really doesn't care much about who I am or what I need: he likes my body, he likes the way we have sex. I need a distraction but I know that seeing him one more time for sex would never be enough. One night where I could forget myself would be nice, though – I miss being touched.

Since I've started going to the meetings I've had

offers from newly sober guys there, but I've enough self-awareness to know that I'm not ready for anything serious. However risky it is, it still feels safer to go back to what I'm familiar with.

I don't see him on the street, no matter how much I will it. Instead I'm soon walking into a grey cement building. I sit halfway back in the crowded room, ready to listen to the speaker share his experience.

As usual I check out who's in the room – it's as much a social place as a time to remind myself why I need to stay away from all substances. A few people share but I'm not really listening. I'm thinking about my letter, lying at the bottom of the post box, wondering if I might be able to get it back.

A well-spoken young woman a few rows ahead of me starts to share. I can't see her face, but what she says grabs my attention.

'I met some new family a few months ago,' she says. 'I have all these sisters – my birth parents, they had got married, I found out. I'm struggling with adapting to it all.'

I crane my neck to see her face: she's a pretty blonde with delicate features. As the meeting ends, I make a direct move towards her.

'Are you adopted?' I ask.

'Yes, it's my birth family that I just met.'

'I was supposed to be at this meeting to hear you,' I tell

her. 'I posted a letter to my birth mother this evening. I'm a wreck, I don't know what to do with myself.'

She is so sweet and encouraging. We exchange phone numbers and as I drive away, I realise I'm noticing signs that I never had before. The threads of hope and trust feel fragile, but in this moment I see that the universe or God, or whatever you want to call it, is supporting me. I, Zara, have let go of self-will for a while and it feels so good.

* * *

It takes three days to get a response, three endless days of trying to distract my mind from going to all the negative places. Three days of staring at walls, unable to have a full conversation as my mind tries to adapt to its new filing system.

I can hear my phone ringing as I unlock the door. Diving onto the bed, I grab it.

'Hello.'

'Zara, it's Ms Cameron. I have some very exciting news. Your mother wants to meet you, but she's going on holiday soon and she also needs to tell her children. She wants to wait to meet you until she gets back in three weeks. She asked if she could write a letter to you first and send photos.'

I'm struggling to absorb her words. I think back to a bizarre memory, how strange it was when I found out that my adoptive parents had not changed their holiday plans when they learned that they could adopt me so as not to disrupt my brother. Instead they paid for my two weeks in foster care. And now my birth mother was also going on a vacation.

'Okay,' I hear myself say a little cautiously. 'You can give her my address. How did she sound? What was her voice like?'

'Oh,' Ms Cameron was gushing again. 'She seems like a lovely warm person. And when she comes back, she wants to meet you – we can set that up. She asked if you would write to her as well.'

'What do I write?'

'Just tell her a little something about yourself, you don't need to tell her your whole life story straight away.'

My heart is literally pounding out of my chest as I put the phone down. In a daze that my birth mother has actually made contact, I start to write on some new pretty pink stationery that my mum gave me, but I feel immediate guilt. It's like I've been stung when I realise the implications and the piece of paper drops from my hand. I choose instead a plain white piece of paper and begin to write. I crumple it up, dissatisfied with the first words my mother will read from me, but a few pages later it feels okay, it feels right. I tell her about a concert I went to and then I spend the rest of the evening trying to decide which photo to send. I even ring James for advice and he mentally runs through the photos he's seen of me over the short time we've been friends. I settle on one of me where I'm wearing a white dress, looking extremely tanned – I look happy and relaxed.

I put it all in an envelope, drop it into the post box with as much strength as I can muster and then go to meet James and Terry for dinner. They can clearly sense my anxiety and I'm glad not to be alone.

'Which photo did you end up sending?' James wants to know.

'The one of me on tour in Australia, where I look sexy.' I sip my hot chocolate.

'Sexy?' Terry laughs out loud. 'You sent a sexy photo to your birth mother?'

I'm laughing now.

'Yes. I have to look good, it's the first time she will have seen me since I was a baby.'

'Zara,' James replies, 'she will love you no matter what you look like. You don't have to worry.'

'I'm not sure about that – I can't think straight most of the time, I can't seem to focus. Is that normal?'

'You're not normal anyway, so yes, it is.' Terry leans in towards me. 'Zara, this is a huge deal: you're going to meet your mother. You're being so brave, stay close to all of us.'

I feel so much warmth as I look at these two men, their handsome faces so loving. I'm feeling luckier by the day.

* * *

Somebody's Daughter

The letter arrives a few days later, in a small white envelope. I take it to my room and lay it on my bed. Her handwriting looks familiar and I realise it's quite similar to mine. I hold the letter up to the light, still sealed, and slowly open it.

18th July 1988
Dear Zara,
Thank you for your letter and photograph. You're a beautiful girl but I knew you would be. You were such a beautiful baby.

I've always hoped that one day you would contact me, but now that it's happened I can't quite believe it. Ever since I spoke to Ms Cameron I can't seem to stop crying.

I felt apprehensive at the thought of meeting this stranger who happens to be my daughter, but on seeing your photograph I can see that you're not a stranger but someone who is very familiar to me.

There is a photo tucked in between the pages. As I hold it up to the light, I'm looking into a young woman's face. She's smiling a little awkwardly and I notice the fullness of her mouth, her straight teeth, her olive skin… *My* skin. Her hair is as dark as mine. I turn the photo around, looking at it from all angles. I still don't know if I look like her, but she looks as familiar to me as she said that I do to her.

As I stare deeper and deeper, my phone starts to ring. I know it's my adopted mum, but I can't answer it. I can't tell her right now. She must never know – it would crush her. Already I'm feeling the burden of my secret, but I don't know what else to do.

I was so interested to hear of your career in the music business.

I would like to try and explain some of the circumstances of your birth as I feel you must want to know.

When I was 16, I was working in the West End. My friend and I used to take days off and go to a club in Wardour Street called 'Les Enfants Terribles'. I met a young Italian man, about 23. (Did you know that you were half-Italian?)

Anyway, we had a brief love affair, which ended in my becoming pregnant. He really wasn't very concerned and as far as I know, he scarpered back to Italy.

You can imagine my parents' shock. 'Nice Jewish girls' just did not get pregnant. I was sent to a mother and baby home in Finchley. After you were born I was meant to stay in the home until you were six weeks old. Unfortunately, the day after I came back I fell ill and I was rushed to the hospital. You were then placed with foster parents and I only saw you once more, when I had to take you to the court to sign the adoption papers.

It's always been my deepest regret that I couldn't keep you, but I was a very immature 17-year-old and without the support of my parents I would never have managed.

I adore my children but there's always been something missing in my life. No child can replace another.

I understand that your parents don't know that you have contacted me. Would they be upset if they knew?

I look forward to hearing from you,

Pat

6

North London, 1970s
and 1980s

Sometimes when I was younger, I would walk holding my mother's hand, looking at the faces of the women that walked past. I would wonder if any of them was the woman who gave birth to me. If I saw anyone that I thought resembled me, I would smile just in case they too saw the similarity. One afternoon I decided that this was the day my mother was going to come and knock on my door and tell me there had been a terrible mistake, or that I was part of an experiment but it was now complete – I had passed the test and now everyone could know each other. I spent that whole day upstairs in our lounge, its big windows overlooking the top of the street. If I stood in a certain position I could see the very top of the hill. She never did come, no matter how much I could almost see her in my mind. When I did dream about my mother I would will myself to look at her face, encourage myself to go ahead and take a look, but her face was always blank.

'Mum,' I ask wistfully the day before my thirteenth birthday, 'do you think she ever thinks about me?'

I notice my mother pause; she knows exactly who I mean, although we rarely speak about it.

'I'm sure she does, especially on your birthday. That must be a very hard day for her.'

I don't answer, now wondering if this is true.

'I will help you look one day, if you like.'

My mother's offer takes me by surprise. Stunned, unsure of what to say, I feel a tingle of excitement in my belly.

'You will?' I answer, my voice hopeful.

'Of course I will,' she says firmly, then pauses. 'But you know, it would devastate me if you did.'

And so the hope left me and I remained, as ever, emotionally tied to her fears and feelings.

* * *

'It's anniversary night,' a young man announces loudly. 'So be quiet, everyone. Oi, calm down, you bunch of drunks!' I'm sitting in a packed AA meeting off the King's Road, the one I attend every week now. It's Saturday night and there's so much energy in the room. I'm sitting in a row with all my new young friends. I feel a comfort from them all, a safety net. I wave and smile at all the people I know, happy in the warmth of the friends I've made.

The man starts calling out the length of time that people have been sober: thirty days, sixty days, ninety days… Each person is met with cheers of encouragement and smiles from the group. I'm able to see the changes easily in other people, the difference between how they look today compared to how they were when they first walked in. It's not just that they are off the drugs and alcohol, it's more than that – a light has taken over them, their faces have changed. It's harder for me to see it in myself, although people tell me I've changed as well.

'And tonight,' the young man bellows again, 'we are also celebrating years. That's right, 365 days of complete and utter sobriety. Is this possible?' He's playing with us, and the crowd responds with hearty cheers.

'With one year of sobriety… Zara! Please come and take your coin and tell us how the fuck you did that!'

The room gets loud; I can see James and Terry beaming. I stand awkwardly at the front of the room. A small cake is being held in front of me with a candle. I stare at its brightness as a huge wave of emotion washes over me and the tears start falling rapidly down my cheeks. I can feel the warmth and love from the room. I know that they understand what this means, the miracle that has taken place for us all. Between sobs, I'm laughing.

Somebody's Daughter

'I never, ever expected that I could do this. And I know that getting a year doesn't mean I'm out of the woods. I'm so grateful for you all.' I look directly at the boys. 'I have never experienced this kind of support and love before. You guys don't care when I'm in a bad mood or being a bitch, you just always say the same thing: keep coming, and don't quit before the miracle. And for the new people...' I look across the room at a young girl sitting at the back, her face pale, eyes sad, and I say to her, 'If I can do this, anyone can. Please keep coming back.'

'Well done, girl!' James hugs me tight. 'Now the fun begins. It's about to get real.'

I pull back to look at his smiling face. 'You're such a wanker!'

'Oh yes, I am, and I hope to be for the rest of my life.'

* * *

The day is here: I'm going to meet the woman who gave birth to me face-to-face. It's been arranged for me to go to Ms Cameron's office in East Finchley. I can walk there. All evening I've obsessed over what to wear to the point where I've driven my friends mad: a dress, jeans, casual, smart?

So I decide on blue jeans, a black top and boots. I put on some make-up and style my hair.

'Zara, she won't care what you wear, she just wants to meet you,' I'd been assured.

Butterflies fill my stomach and I'm finding it hard to

breathe. She is bringing her husband, as I said that was okay. I had decided not to take anyone with me, but now I wonder if that was a huge mistake. The end of August sunlight is trying to push through the clouds as I walk slowly up the street. I have this desire to grab a passer-by, a man that rushes past me. I want to stop him and tell him where I'm going, what I'm about to do, but I don't – I feel almost envious towards anyone having a regular day.

The grey building is in the distance. I walk to the door and up the stairs, panic rising inside me as I see Ms Cameron, who somehow knows I have arrived. She guides me gently up the stairs, but I'm not ready.

'Your mother is here already. Dear, it's okay.' She sees my face, hears my rapid breathing. I feel like I'm going to have a panic attack.

'I can't do this, I *can't*.'

My words are quiet; did she hear me? I turn around but my back is against the door. It's too late. She opens it, and turns me around. A man is standing in front of me, crying. I look past him and see my mother sitting on a chair – she doesn't get up. She is petite, ladylike, neat and well groomed. What do I do? She has tears in her eyes, but they're not falling onto her cheeks like mine. Her husband, unashamed to show his emotion, moves towards me and kisses me on each cheek. I turn to my mother. *Am I supposed to approach her?* She does not stand as I lean in and kiss her cheek. She's controlled, far more than me.

I sink into an armchair, grateful for its comfort, and find myself unable to speak. I'm staring at her, every part of her body: her face, her nose, her lips, her hands… I take in all of it. She is familiar, her features seem magnified to me; I see myself in her.

She and Ms Cameron begin to chat but I'm not listening – I'm staring, I can't stop staring. Is she pretty? I'm not sure. Do I look like her? I can't tell. She is familiar, so familiar; a stranger, but someone I know.

I notice that my tears have stopped while I'm comparing boobs. I'm stunned by my own shallowness and the way my mind is working right now. *How come her boobs are bigger than mine? Her legs are mine, my legs on another person.* She is wearing clothes that I would wear.

She wears silver jewellery. My adoptive mother wears gold, but I wear silver. She is young and trendy; I like that. My adoptive mother takes pride in her clothes, but they were never clothes I would borrow. I would borrow this mother's clothes, and they would fit for she is slim like me. I'm filled with guilt at being happy that she is slim.

I feel guilty just for being there.

I start to feel more relaxed and start talking but I can't remember what is being said to me. I can't stop staring. By the end of the meeting we have made a plan for me to go and meet my siblings – a sixteen-year-old sister and a thirteen-year-old brother, who now know of my existence and are very excited to meet me. I like hearing about them. I've gone from being the youngest in my family to the oldest in this new one.

Later that afternoon, I find myself driving towards my adoptive mother's house. No one is home but I have a key. I go into her bedroom and I sit on the floor of her dressing room. I breathe in the scent of her familiar, comforting perfume. I sit there for what seems like a very long time and I stare at the walls.

* * *

Pat opens the door to her house. She had given me directions, but I didn't tell her that I knew the way already, that I had sat outside spying on her, waiting for a glimpse of her. My sister is standing with her mother, *our* mother. She is smiling; I embrace her. We both laugh. My brother is in the kitchen, sitting on the counter, his hands covering his face. I think he's crying, and soon I start to cry too.

The aunts and uncles are arriving, all bearing presents for me as if I've just been born. These are the ones who helped Pat, letting her hide in their homes while she was pregnant. I don't know what to do except cry as they hand me more gifts. I feel like I'm some kind of oddity, or a prodigal daughter, or maybe a singing star.

Somebody's Daughter

'I watched *Top of the Pops*. I saw you with Nick Kamen, I remember that outfit,' my sister says as I show them the photo albums I've brought along. I see the similarity in our faces, but she seems to favour her father more than she does me.

It's not easy for Pat, looking at the photos of me as a baby and a little girl. I see her trying to hide her tears. She is looking closely at each photo; she seems to have shut down. I understand, for I have done the same thing my whole life when things have felt too difficult.

Now it's my turn to look through albums, with my mother and sister next to me on the sofa. Our legs touch, connecting us all. They laugh at their photos, sharing memories, showing me how cute they were as babies and small children. I look, taking in the images; a sadness, mingled with joy, seems to flow back and forth between us.

I watch my siblings with their mother, *our* mother. That's going to take some time for me to get used to. They're showing off, climbing on their mum. I stay seated on the sofa, laughing as I watch them. I see the connection they have, the bond created by growing up together. Do I have that with my family, with my mother? Maybe I do and I just can't see it, but it's never felt that it flowed as easily as this. I know I'll never have that with them – or will I? In time, maybe?

Enjoy it, Zara, I'm saying inside my head, *look at them, this is what you've been looking for.* I push down the wave of grief that I feel, hoping they cannot sense it.

My grandparents have arrived. I don't know how to greet them. My grandfather is looking me up and down. I finally stand in front of him. He's not much taller than me, but slim. 'So, you're the skeleton in our closet.' He is laughing but I'm not sure I find that comment as funny as he does.

My grandmother can't speak to me at all. She avoids eye contact, yet every time I look up, I see her staring. I'm aware that she's watching me closely, taking me in the same way I'm taking them in.

So here I am. I have fantasised about these people for so long, as is common for people like me. I'm surrounded by this other Jewish family that in some ways is not so different to the one I was raised in: silent grandparents with stifled emotions, little old Jewish men, kind and funny. These are my uncles, my relatives, and I see pieces of my face in all of them.

Pat is young and glamorous, eighteen years younger than Mum. She has invited me to look in her new walk-in closet. I like her clothes and her jewellery. We're bonding over clothes because it's safer to talk about them than anything else. I feel guilty for being pleased that my birth mother dresses this way – I know my adopted mum could never compete. They are two very different women, from different generations. My new grandparents remind me more of my parents' generation; Pat feels like more of a big sister than a mother. Enamoured, I make notes of what she wears in my head.

My sister has not left my side. She follows me around like a puppy dog while my thirteen-year-old brother just stares like my grandma. I'm the centre of this complex situation, with these strangers to whom I happen to be genetically related.

I say goodbye as it's almost getting dark. A light rain is in the air and exhaustion has taken over me. They all come out, my new family, standing on the doorstep smiling and waving me off. I smile back. Somehow I manage to drive on to the motorway before the howl erupts that I have kept contained all day. It comes from deep inside of me. I can no longer keep this under control. There are no drugs to push it down anymore. I know now what I have been running from. The tears are flooding my face, making it hard to drive, but I don't pull off the road – I just keep going, sobbing just like that broken-hearted little girl did before she started running from herself. My shoulders shake as I let it pass through me.

* * *

I watch my adoptive mother in the kitchen – she loves to cook. A big pot of chicken soup sits on the stove.

'You want some *kneidlach*? How many? Two, three?'

She is rolling the dumplings and placing them in the bubbling soup.

'Two, please,' I respond, leaning against the door.

'You hungry?' she asks.

I nod. She cuts me a thick piece of Cheddar cheese.

'I'm not supposed to eat it, but you can. It's delicious.'

I smile and take it from her, leaning against the doorway.

Mum hums while she works, her mood upbeat. She's an interesting conundrum, one moment as solid and strong as an anchor and yet when she feels criticised she falls to the ground, angry and hurt. And then within the next moment she is back to herself. I have always found the way she behaves confusing, my mind unable to adjust to her rapid change of pace. One time when I was little, I stood by her dressing-room door secretly and watched as she slapped and punched herself, saying out loud how stupid she was. It scared me to see her that way, but it showed me who she was underneath it all.

I still haven't told her about meeting Pat, although it has been a few months. I spent Christmas Day having lunch with my adoptive family and then dinner with my birth family. I'm still consumed with guilt and the feeling that I must protect her.

'But Zara, she's a grown-up,' my friends tell me. 'It's not your responsibility.' But that doesn't help me at all.

It's becoming clearer to me the panic I feel is not all about her, it's also about the possibility that she may reject me for finding my birth mother. I would not be able to cope without her. It seems the three of us – my birth mother, adopted mother and me – are all scared of the same thing.

I'm so grateful for my music right now. Endless songs of reunion and staying clean are being written in this new band that I'm in. I like being around the sober guys, although we are all rather nuts. We're doing so many gigs in London, and more people are showing up; we're recording every day. I have very little money but I'm beginning to feel a sense of freedom that I haven't really felt before.

* * *

It's 5am and I'm lying awake. I need to tell my adoptive parents that I've found her. Two years of living this double life, running from one family to another, have passed. I can't contain it anymore. Living this split life has taken its toll, with the constant fear that my adopted mum will somehow find out.

I call my friend: 'I need to tell them today, I feel sick.' I'm finding myself near hysteria, but he calms me with his low, rich voice.

I dial my mum's number and she answers. I'm crying already.

'Mum, I need to come over and tell you something.'

I pull into the driveway. My mother looks so worried. I

realise then that I should never have scared her in this way.

'I found my birth mother a long time ago. I never told you because I didn't want to hurt you, but I can't live with this secret anymore.' There, it's out, I've said it. The whole time my father has been sitting on the sofa, staring at the floor. He doesn't say a word.

My mother too is silent for a moment. 'Well, I don't know why you didn't tell me. I wouldn't have minded, I always told you that.' She is finding something to do, shuffling papers on the table. 'So, what is she like then? That woman? Do you have a photo?'

'Yes, Mum, I do.' I had decided before on bringing just a couple of photos and my instinct is right; she only wants to see one.

'She looks very nice. And this is your sister?'

'Yes, Mum – Roberta.'

'Well, obviously you want to be in touch with her. Your sister is much more important to have a relationship with than that woman.'

I do what I always do, without faltering: 'Of course, Mum, she's more important to me than Pat.'

'And the father?' Mum questions.

'Just a first name, Mum, nothing more. But I'm Italian.'

'Yes, dear, we knew that. But I wouldn't give it much thought.'

My stomach has tightened in disbelief: they knew. They

had always known… The time when my mother was upset with me for bringing a cross back from the Vatican now made sense; as a little girl being talked to in Italian by people on holiday. Was that the reason why? Did she somehow think my Italian side would overshadow my Jewishness?

My father still stares at the ground. He has still not uttered one word. I leave, apologising for the way I did this.

I feel like a weight has been lifted from my shoulders.

* * *

A couple of days later, I'm calling my birth mother.

'Pat, I need to know who my father is,' I say. My voice is shaking as I hold the phone.

'I've told you everything I know. Why do you care about him? It's me that went through it all, he didn't care about you.' She is angry, but I can't stop pushing.

'I need to know, Pat. It's important to me.'

'Why? Other adopted people don't care, I know many who are satisfied with finding their mothers. Am I not enough for you?' She's furious.

I'm struggling, in a state of shock. I hadn't anticipated this – I had thought that after meeting one's mother, they would support you.

'Zara, you're triggering her past,' my adopted friend from the 12-step meeting said. 'She's struggling too – you need to be patient.'

But I'm not feeling patient; I'm back battling with that familiar rage. It burns inside me. I feel out of control and I want to use something. I'm tired of walking on eggshells, I'm tired of protecting everyone. There is a handsome man at the meeting, and he is perfect for me right now.

* * *

I receive a letter from Pat, saying she can't deal with my anger; that I need to accept that she doesn't know anything more about my father, and that it's not her place to try and find him. I write hurriedly that I have had enough of her blaming me for her past. We are both spewing venom, the honeymoon period over.

My anger about my childhood has erupted. I know I blame my birth mother for what happened in my home. I want her to say she's sorry that she gave me away. I want to hear the words, but the more I push the angrier she gets. She does not want to understand my childhood, it's too painful for her. She refuses to see me and writes that if I won't accept the situation the way it is then I cannot see her children either. I'm trying to explain that I don't want to argue, that I just need some time, but it's all or nothing: we don't speak for a couple of years.

* * *

I have my first using dream. I'm in a dark room, lying in a

bed naked with a man that I don't recognise. The sheets are stained a dull red, but I know it's not blood. I'm burning cocaine on tin foil, or is it my brother's heroin? I inhale a large amount and feel it burning in my chest. The man offers me a joint and I take it hungrily. Dull, grey smoke fills the room. My head is swimming. I fall back onto the bed as he moves on top of me. I wake up…

For one small second, I'm not sure if it's real or not. The relief when I realise it was a dream is palpable. I turn on my bedroom light and ring James.

'I had this awful dream, it was so real,' I tell him before I even say hello. 'I felt that I was using, that I was back there. I can't seem to shake it off – I had sex and everything.'

'Sounds marvellous,' he responds, laughing.

'James, it was insane. Why am I dreaming about this?'

'It's just a reminder, girl. It's a drunk dream, that's all. Just get to more meetings and share about it. I would say that you need to get laid, but I think you've had your fair share of that for a few years.'

'James! Me? I'm pure as the driven snow, you know that.' I'm laughing again, back in the moment. 'But what do I do about Pat? It feels so awful, I feel so rejected again. I don't know how to move through all of this.'

'Zara, you have to trust. Give her space, give yourself time. Patience is what's needed. You're doing well, girl. That's all you need to worry about right now.'

I'm still split. I feel the impossibility of living two lives, having two identities.

'You must feel relieved, you must feel whole again, complete,' people say to me and I find that I have no words, no answers. It's just like when I was a small child and people used to tell me how lucky I was to be adopted. I still don't feel lucky, and I don't know how to answer them.

But I'm managing to disassociate myself from Pat not being in touch with me. I go back to a time before I knew her; I find myself saying I could cope back then, and I can cope just fine now. I pretend that I still don't know who she is, but it's hard to close that door completely. I'm floating in the wind, grabbing onto a man to fix me, to anchor me, but none of it works.

My adopted mother and I are arguing even more. Is it sobriety that's making me so unable to accept who they are? I've lost my tolerance for the fact that they choose to bury their heads in the sand. I'm angry that I have to look at myself, I'm angry at who they are, and who they're not.

I know I want her to carry it all. I have always wanted her to know what the weight feels like, the way it presses and weighs down on me like a huge grey ship carrying its heavy over-spilling cargo to the bottom of the ocean. But she has always been unable to be my safety net, or carry much of this burden for she has had her own.

'Why me?' I say, full of self-pity.

'Because it has to be you. Your life depends upon it,' I am told.

'Fuck that!' I snap back. But I know they're right: no matter how much I bitch and moan, I'm feeling stronger.

I dive into singing more. I have another gig, this time with David Essex, a man that I used to have a poster of on my bedroom wall. I'm back on *Top of the Pops*. This time I have a clearer head and I enjoy every moment. I write songs, I sing, because it helps me cope with my emotions. I'm so grateful for this gift. I know now that it didn't come from my birth mother, so perhaps it came from my father?

My fantasy mother that I had thought about all my life had been turned to reality. The nurturing woman who would love me completely is not real: she has her own pain and I'm a reminder of it. All I can do is focus on myself, I can't change the pain that happened to us. I'm not religious, but I'm finding comfort in sources outside myself.

A handsome man in AA has my attention. He's American. We start to date, and for once I don't have sex immediately, I get to know him first. Then I realise how much I want to be a mother, but he's not ready and leaves. I'm catapulted backwards into that sea of separation and panic; I can't do this anymore.

* * *

It seems to take months of soul-searching to find that peaceful place within myself, the one that always seems slightly out of reach.

'Just think of yourself as a big onion,' Terry says. 'Layer after layer unravelling. That's what this is all about, getting to know ourselves.'

'You and James seem a bit obsessed with this onion analogy. Will I end up smelling like one too?'

'You already do, Zara – didn't you know? Everyone in the meetings always comments.' He always makes me giggle, no matter how silly our conversations are.

I have a ticket to go to LA for a week and visit a sober friend who just moved there. I'm excited as I get off the plane.

America, here I am.

Everything looks so different; the sky feels vaster. There seems to be more space to breathe. I feel the weight fall away. I feel a sense of freedom. The time is good for me to absorb all that has taken place.

I head to a 12-step meeting and meet a group of young people. They are warm and welcoming, amongst them a handsome, clean-looking man. He is sober; he has a sparkle in his eyes and a kindness to his outgoing personality. I'm drawn to him, but curious. We spend a few days hanging out. I feel quite shy around these people – they ask so many questions and as I tell them a little of my story I can feel the build-up of tears, but I push it down, surprised by my vulnerability.

Somebody's Daughter

'You met someone,' Cassie says, the day after I get home. She's sitting on my floor, drinking tea. 'Hold on, let me tell you what I get.'

'What you get?' I answer. 'Oh, for fuck's sake, what have you been doing while I was away?'

'I've been doing some psychic training with this incredible man.'

'Oh, that's what you're calling it, are you – psychic training?' I laugh.

I almost roll my eyes when she stands up, stretches her arms out wide, looking to the sky. But my mouth is wide open.

'What?' I ask.

'I don't know why I'm doing this,' Cassie replies.

'Kevin does that all the time – he trained as an actor. It's an exercise from some famous teacher, Chekhov, he showed me this exercise one evening. Bloody hell, I can't believe you got that!'

'You're going to marry him,' Cassie says, smiling.

* * *

Kevin writes and calls me often. He's quite a serious guy, very committed to his recovery, and I like that about him. He seems so grounded that I open up to him. I feel like I'm on this rollercoaster ride and I can't get off. The universe is urging me, pushing me to go to LA – I stop fighting it.

Within six months I know I have to get away from here: I need space from my two families. I need to find myself again and find out if what I have with this man is real. So I write to Pat, who I still have not heard from, to tell her I'm leaving. She calls me and we say nothing about the time spent apart. I feel better knowing we're back in touch. I tell my adoptive mother and she encourages me to go to LA – we both know it's the only way our relationship can work, it's not that we don't love each other.

I book a one-way ticket and head for Los Angeles, holding in my hand the most beautiful letter my adoptive mother has ever written to me.

7

Los Angeles, 1996

'Hey, pretty lady! What you got in that big old belly of yours, a boy or a girl?'

His accent is thick, southern, which is unusual in Los Angeles. He's a handsome stranger, smiling at me in the bookstore.

'I don't know, I didn't want to find out, but my sense is it's a boy.' I rub my stomach automatically.

'The father is a lucky man. You're a pretty one and I love your accent, so delicious!'

I find myself blushing at his frankness, surprised that any man would be looking at me in that way right now. These days I can barely see my feet and I move awkwardly between the bookcases, trying to judge the distance. I spend hours here, trying to pass the time. Mostly I look at pregnancy books, enjoying seeing photos of the stages my baby is progressing through. I cannot work – my immigration papers are still not finalised. I have few friends as I have only lived here less than a year.

After meeting Kevin I had decided to stay in Los Angeles to really give it a go. I knew I wanted a family, and he did too. This was my chance and I wasn't going to let fear stop me, I felt. Kevin was different to the other men that I'd been wasting my time on: he had a steady job and he wasn't a womaniser the way my previous boyfriends had been. I felt safe with him and he seemed to take pride in looking after me and being the stable one. He liked being in control emotionally and so far it worked for me. I still felt so unsure of myself. I knew that I was dependent on him, but it felt lovely to have a man who genuinely cared about my wellbeing; we are starting a family together.

We had gone back to England to get married. My adoptive mum was finally proud and excited that I was doing something all her friends' children had done. I wasn't allowed to invite Pat to the wedding but I didn't fight it – I was more than ready to move on with my own life. Six weeks later, I was pregnant.

'Goodbye, English lady. I hope I see you again someday.'

I have made some new friends in my pregnancy exercise class. I love being around all these women – we make fun of each other as our bellies grow and it's harder to get up off the floor.

I have never been around pregnant women before, nor had any real conversation about what it means to be pregnant. As far as I can remember, my adoptive mother never had any pregnant friends. I have rarely been around a newborn baby. That does not scare me, though. I have always loved babies; drawn to them like magnets, and them to me. I'm the one they wave at as I walk past them in a restaurant.

After smiling back at the man, I then walk outside into the hot LA sunshine. I slide into my car and drive home.

As I nap that afternoon, feeling my baby moving inside me, I dream. I'm in a hospital, no longer pregnant; I walk steadily up to the reception desk.

'I've come to pick up my baby. I gave birth to him last night.'

The nurse looks at me quizzically. As she reaches for the phone, I wake up.

The dreams continue as I get closer to my due date: I'm always going to collect him, I never give birth in my dreams. The dreams seem to be getting more intense and I worry that Kevin is finding all this too much. I'm being woken up in the night now by what I can only describe as a great big boulder in my stomach that's trying to escape. My emotions are so tangled and huge that they feel like a separate entity. No longer able to contain the grief anymore,

Somebody's Daughter

I wake up and start to howl. In many ways it's a relief. I see myself whizzing down a tunnel, further and further. I stop myself by jumping out of bed.

'Zara, I think you just need to keep going, let the feelings out,' says Kevin. 'Then maybe it will stop.'

'I can't do that. I don't understand why this keeps happening, I want it to stop,' I insist.

'Let me hold you,' Kevin says kindly.

'No, I can't. Thank you, but no.'

He looks sad – I know he's trying to help me.

'I think you sound like a baby when you cry. This is connected to you being given up. You know that, right?' he says. 'You need to talk to your therapist about this.'

I knew he was right, but I was feeling angry again – I don't like being under a microscope. I do call my therapist, though. Also an adopted person, she explains to me about cellular memory.

'The body remembers before there are words. It's just your body letting you know it's time to release all those feelings that you have held on to for so long. It won't kill you, Zara, just let it happen. I promise you it will pass.'

'I'm worried about my baby feeling all of this,' I say quietly.

'Talk to your baby, tell him what's going on,' she says reassuringly.

She believes me when I say it's a him. I don't know how I

know, it's a feeling inside. I know his personality already; I know my baby and I can't explain how.

Did my mother know me?

So I run myself a hot bath. My ribs are sore from this little person moving and stretching inside me. I feel him move again, seeing the shape of a foot or a hand pressed against the inside of my stomach.

'Hi, little baby. It's me, your mama. I'm so excited to meet you, I can barely wait, but listen,' I whisper, 'Mama had a weird start. My mother had to give me away after she gave birth to me and for some strange reason I'm feeling it all and acting a bit crazy emotionally. Or it could just be my hormones.' I rub my belly gently. 'But I want you to know that you will never ever be separated from me. I'm going to probably drive you crazy and when I cry it's not about you, my darling. You're already filling me with so much joy, so please be patient.'

As I close my eyes, I sink deeper into the bath. I feel pure excitement rise in my stomach at the thought that this little person would be with us very soon.

* * *

I push through the ring of fire; I burn inside. I'm amazed at what my body is capable of. The pain spirals throughout me. I'm focused, in the moment, giving everything I have. I'm pushing, but he won't come out. The doctor is worried,

I can tell. I push harder. I'm exhausted, sweating. Finally, with the doctor yelling at me to keep going, I push this little boy into the world. He's so beautiful, I can't take my eyes off him.

'Don't leave him with anyone,' I tell my husband as they go to bathe him. 'Do you understand? No one can take him out of the room. You hold him.'

I haven't slept, but I feel awake, already getting used to the feel of my body without the baby inside.

Kevin beams proudly and walks off with the baby as if he's been holding him for many years. I'm anxiously waiting for him to return as soon as they've left. When they do, I hold this tiny little boy in my arms and immediately he nurses – I have never felt so much love for anyone in my life.

I think about Pat, and how she never got to say goodbye to me when I was born. I can't let the thought linger, it makes me want to vomit. So I hold my baby tighter. I realise then the only way that a woman can truly survive in that situation is to disassociate herself far away enough to cope. My heart is wide open. Every wall that I have so tirelessly built around me crumpled the moment he took his first breath; I feel a new strength within me. I have created a life – I gave birth the same way millions of women have done before me. I feel a connection to the ghosts of them all. I stay awake all night, staring at him.

* * *

Kevin and I are both exhausted. It doesn't help that the nightmares have now started again. I try to sleep, but my dreams are filled with visions of my baby disappearing, someone trying to steal him. I have not told Kevin as I worry he will want to have me locked up, but it all just reinforces how little he really knows about my inner life. I've never allowed anyone to truly see it all.

I can't leave the baby alone for a moment – I have this feeling that if I walk out of the room he will vanish, never to be found again. I've bought a sling and tell Kevin that it's better for the baby to be carried at all times. But it's for me really: I need to be next to him, to know he won't leave. I'm so tired, I can't stop crying. I think briefly for a moment about seeking oblivion with a drink or drugs. I feel myself slipping back to my childhood state, where all the instability of my family's emotions left me so deeply raw, with a constant loneliness. It was an ache that could never be healed.

A friend of ours suggests I may have post-natal depression and maybe he's right, but my therapist disagrees. 'Zara, it's just the grief that's all, you're finally allowing yourself to grieve and when you do, you will start healing,' she tells me.

'Zara,' Kevin says, 'you can't stay awake all night guarding the baby, you need to sleep.' But I can't help myself – I can't sleep. I'm on high alert, getting used to being a mother, getting used to living with someone who's related to me for the first time.

Somebody's Daughter

In spite of all those intense feelings, I have brief moments of peace. Sometimes I feel as if my whole life were all leading up to this one point. Our son Samuel is so sweet, the way he coos at me. I can see in his eyes he wants to smile, but I have to wait another week until that magnificent moment comes. But I feel lonely in my cocoon, longing for family to be around me when my husband is away working long hours. I want to show my baby off to everyone. I want my mum. Then I think it's better that Kevin works so much, so he can't see all of me. If he did, I'm sure he would realise his mistake. I'm spending most of my day making up songs that Samuel has to listen to – I think he likes them, I see his eyes shining.

'Zara, I'm coming to visit now,' says my mother over the phone. 'You've had enough time to get into a routine. I'm leaving your father at home.' As soon as I hear her voice I shut down. I crave her presence, yet I'm worried too.

She arrives, as she always does, in a wheelchair. It's not that my mother cannot walk, just that she finds airports too hard to walk through and lives for the attention. I feel criticised the moment she walks in the house.

'I don't like your pots, those handles get way too hot. Is this the only utensil you have for frying?' She is busy already, organising the kitchen. 'You're not still nursing that baby, are you? Sleeping with him? That's not healthy, Zara.' I try to keep my mouth shut, but it's hard – I feel stifled and worried about the week ahead. I don't tell her the truth: that I can't leave my baby in a room for fear he will vanish into thin air. I don't mention the nightmares either. I'm also aware, as she watches me nursing him, she herself never had this opportunity. I feel sad for her and almost apologetic that I could have a child so easily when she tried so hard for many years. I look at her warmly.

I desperately want to say, 'Mum, if I could, I would do anything for you to experience this. I know you wanted it, I'm so sorry.' But I don't say a word.

'Zara, for goodness' sake when are you going to stop taking it all on board? You feel guilty for everything,' Kevin says to me that night. I know he's right.

We go swimming in the morning and I let Mum hold Samuel. He lies across her chest, sleeping peacefully. My mum looks so content. I feel a wave of sadness. I wish we didn't live so far apart, but I also know it's for the best: our relationship will last longer this way. On the last day I cry as she leaves. I'm torn again – I want my mother but I feel suffocated by her at the same time.

8

Los Angeles, 1999

C assie, my childhood friend from back home, is chatting to me on the phone as I lie in the sun in our back garden. Samuel is almost three. He has a friend over and I watch as the two little boys run back and forth through the sprinklers.

'I'm leaving Frank. We haven't had sex in seven years, it's ridiculous! What kind of a marriage is that?' She never says 'hello'.

'I thought you were going to do it when you were on holiday,' I say, moving to sit in the shade.

'Oh, we tried. I drank three glasses of champagne to get the courage to attempt to seduce him, but he would only get undressed in the dark. I fell sideways off the bed trying to find him and went mad. I couldn't stop yelling. I need to find someone to shag.'

I laugh out loud. 'Well, at least you tried. I myself am cured of men problems. I will never look at another man – my baby boy is all I need. The desire to stray has gone forever.'

'It's gone for now because you just pushed an eight-pound baby out your whatsit! You will feel womanly again.'

'I really won't. I think I'm cured, seriously. Try it, it works.' But I wasn't being truly honest. I still thought about him from time to time. I imagine reaching out and calling, but something stops me.

Samuel talks a lot. I love hearing how his speech develops, words that join together and then a sentence. He's a happy boy, and so inquisitive. I don't want to be apart from him if I can help it. All I need is an hour here and there to recharge.

Samuel was already getting so big and was three years old when I became pregnant again. But eight weeks in, no heartbeat was found. Devastated, I fall into a depression. I tell my adoptive mother as soon as it happens.

'At least you've one baby already,' she says. But I know what she's saying in between the lines: my mother had several miscarriages but we had never talked about her infertility.

'Mum, I can't imagine what that must have been like for you,' I find myself saying tentatively.

'It made me feel like I wasn't a woman. A proper woman.' She lets out a hollow laugh.

I'm stunned by her honesty, and feel a pain deep inside my heart. I wish that she too could experience pregnancy and childbirth. A wave of compassion flows through me. It has taken many years to get here, but finally we have connected through a common loss. It has taken this to feel it.

I'm desperate to get pregnant again, to take away the pain – it's like the rug has been pulled out from beneath me. I never expected this to happen. I carry around a statue of an angel of fertility that a friend gave me. I imagine a pomegranate tree bursting with fruit. At night, as I close my eyes I see a little girl's round face with long straight hair and a beautiful smile. She visits me often, but I don't say a word to anyone about her.

Kevin is patient and kind. He keeps telling me not to worry, he is sure I will get pregnant again. I make him have sex with me all the time. He's getting exhausted. I see him also getting tired of my neediness.

'I wish I thought you wanted to have sex with me, but I know you don't. I think it's just for a baby.' He looks serious as I lie back, legs up in the air – I had read that this would help me conceive. I feel bad, but it doesn't come out gently.

'Kevin, you want more children, don't you?' He nods. 'So that's why we're doing this. It has to be done this way when I'm ovulating. We need to have sex every day right now, most men would be happy.'

'Not like this. I feel like a machine,' he says. I study his face. I know in some ways he is right. The cracks are already beginning to show, but I ignore them.

Kevin's mood suddenly changes. He reaches over and grabs me by the feet, pulling my legs up in the air. He shakes me hard until we both start to giggle. Rolling over, we kiss gently.

'You want another baby with me?' he asks gently.

'Yes, please.'

* * *

I sit outside in the heat beside Samuel, burying the baby book I had started writing beneath a new tree we had planted. I still feel so sad, but also shocked – I never thought this could happen to me.

'She will come back again, Mummy,' my little boy says, laying his hand gently on my knee.

I'm quiet, feeling his sweetness. 'Who are you, Moses?' I'm finally laughing.

'I'm not Moses, I'm Samuel.' He pats himself on the chest.

'Are you sure?' I joke. 'You sound like a prophet to me.'

'I am me, Mama. Don't worry.' His little hand reaches over and touches my cheek.

I decide to go to an adoption conference after being advised to do so by my therapist. I had started seeing her when I first got married, it was suggested by a friend as an investment in our relationship. She feels that it would be helpful to me to

114

know that I'm not the only adopted person in the world who feels the way I do. I'm nervous as I walk in and hold my breath as I listen. I'm struck by the commonalities: they talk like me, I'm not alone. I find a support group and start making some fabulous new friends. Immediately I feel at home, the same way I did when I walked into my first 12-step meeting all those years ago. This is what I've needed. I'm savouring every word, soaking it all in like a tiny sponge. I can finally speak my truth without explaining – they understand, they live with the same feelings. I am home.

'Zara, you have to forgive yourself for not being the right daughter for your mother,' one of the speakers tells me.

I can't seem to answer her. No one has ever said this to me before. These people understand the inside of my head.

'It's not your fault, now is it? The fact that you're so different?'

They are teaching me to look at things in a different light and I feel a sense of relief: I've carried so much shame about my behaviour towards my adoptive mother. I've been so confused as to why we don't connect, especially when I know she wants to as much as I do. I've felt I had a piece missing that I could never resolve, yet as a mother I have no problem being connected to my babies. I'm also learning it's not my fault, it's all down to circumstance. I hope that once I understand it all, things will change.

* * *

Somebody's Daughter

I'm finally pregnant again and things are progressing well. I am enjoying all the things we get to do as mothers, all the school plays, the trips and activities. Kevin and I co- parent well most of the time but I know he is also frustrated with me. It seems all of my 'stuff', as we call it, is just being highlighted in this relationship. I knew that living with someone would push me to new ways of revealing myself, but I feel like I'm a tortoise that retreats into his shell. I need that time to myself, but sometimes Kevin takes it as a rejection. When he does, instead of being able to reach for him, I start feeling suffocated and he loses me even more.

'Why can't you meet me halfway? Why do you always busy yourself to avoid me?'

I don't know the answer so I bluff.

'I talk to you, it's not like I avoid you,' I say, but I'm painfully aware that I change the conversation when things feel too heavy. 'It's all a bit of a commitment, that's all,' I add. I'm serious, but Kevin is howling with laughter.

'Zara, we're married and we have a child together, with another on the way! You make no sense.'

I laugh back.

'It makes perfect sense to me,' I tell him.

I'm smiling at him as he rolls his eyes. He pulls me close and I allow myself to sink into his arms. He moves back, looking into my eyes. I find I'm doing the same thing with him as I did with my mother: I don't like it when he's angry with me so I have to make it right. And when we are close, I pull away.

'I am here for you forever. I'm never going anywhere. You know that, don't you?' He looks at me gently.

'Yes, yes, yes!'

I'm still making fun of him but the words are comforting – I feel safe.

* * *

I'm lying on the sofa, nursing our few-months-old baby daughter, Katie. She finally came to me and it has filled me with love once more, even if my breasts are so full of milk they ache. I squeeze her chubby little thighs and watch Kevin fix dinner, talking away to Samuel, taking in this domestic scene.

Kevin is straight in so many ways – I think that's what drew me to him, I liked the stability. Sex for him must only be about love, and done in a loving way. I'm not used to that. I have told him some parts of my life but he doesn't want to hear it all. It's apparent that I've had more partners and more experiences than him. He seems to think that he can dip me in holy water and wash all of that away. But I still think about my past. My old life is never far from my thoughts, no matter how much I love him and our babies.

I still dream of Simon sometimes and wake up surprised that he is in my thoughts. Occasionally I will hear a titbit from a friend in London, telling me news of him. I have stayed away for years. I keep my dreams a secret; I still like secrets. I don't really know if I can live without any at all.

I wish for a storm as I listen to my son's questions. It's so hot and dry I find it stifling. How I miss the dewy air in London – I miss everything about home. Sometimes I see the smog sitting on the horizon and I feel suffocated, but Kevin always gets upset if I say anything too negative: he knows I miss home but it's hard for him to accept. Today there's a fire on the mountain in front of our house. I can see it through the kitchen window as I do the washing-up.

'You can't go outside today, Samuel. There's ash falling from the sky. It's not good for you to breathe.'

Samuel is dressed as Batman – he has been wearing the same costume for four months straight now.

'I am Batman, not Samuel.' He darts between the chairs. 'Batman can inhale ash.'

'Batman really shouldn't,' I say, putting the baby in her high chair and turning back to the sink. 'Even superheroes need to breathe clean air. Samuel!' I yell. 'Take that mask off the baby, she doesn't want to be Robin.'

The caped crusader runs out the room. I can hear him laughing as I take the mask off the baby.

I make some adaptations to Samuel's costume – a moustache he asked me to paint on and more scars drawn down his cheek to prove he went into battle. It's the only way I can get him to take the mask off – the heat in LA isn't good for a little boy in a mask.

I see people staring at my superhero and me as we walk, side by side, into the grocery store, but I'm not embarrassed. Each day I feel more pride at these little human beings I have created. I find it easy to enhance my imagination; I'm perfectly comfortable living there right alongside them.

My life is full of noise. Every waking moment someone needs something. The clothes that pile up on the floor don't wash themselves and some days I don't even manage to get dressed. Other mothers seem to look so perfect. They fascinate me. When do they get their make-up on? But I love being a mother despite the fatigue and find peace in it all once again. It helps put those thoughts to the back of my mind. It's easy to pack everything up for a little while as I've always done.

* * *

11 September 2001. I'm driving Samuel to school. He's not allowed to wear a costume but the teacher agreed to allow a cape attached to his T-shirt. Then I get the call that the Twin Towers are falling. My friend Julie is yelling down the phone. I can't understand her. How can this be possible? I turn on the radio, quiet so Samuel can't hear. Should I turn back? As I pull in, the parents are standing around, shell-shocked. The school assures me that it's safe to leave

Samuel, but I'm so afraid – we don't know what's going to happen next.

We all struggle to comprehend what has happened. I spend the morning with Katie, playing and watching television, but I'm really just counting the minutes until it's time for me to get Samuel. I keep trying to call my adopted mum but the lines to London are down. That night I can't sleep. My dreams are interwoven with terror and images of those people jumping out of the buildings; I don't think I have ever felt so afraid. My baby girl looks at me so seriously, like she knows something is wrong. I turn off the news when Samuel is around – I want to protect my children for as long as I can.

There are no planes in the sky even though we live near an airport. I miss their sound. It feels like we're in a horror movie, nothing feels the same. I feel closer to Kevin, though – we're warmer to one another and we talk more. One night, we make love on the living-room floor while the children are sleeping in our bed. Our third child is conceived. The world changes for us once more.

A few months later, I'm reading an article about how many pregnancies happened after 9/11. All the couples say they weren't planning it, but after any great tragedy there is an influx in pregnancies. These little souls are replenishing the world. As the days roll on, as we all try and adjust to the new normal, this new world.

'Can you make sure it's a boy?' Samuel asks seriously as my belly swells again. He pats my stomach gently.

'I'll try my best, but I don't have much say.'

'Who does?' he asks.

'God does, and the eggs inside.'

I'm chasing Katie, who is giggling – I'm trying to get her clothes on.

'Can you ask God and the eggs?'

'I will, but I can't promise anything.'

My breathing is shallow, the baby already moving inside me as I tackle Katie to the ground. My baby girl won't sleep in a crib, she shakes the bars as if they are the gates of jail so we all sleep in bed together.

Kevin is working a lot. He is a film editor and his hours are long. I know the stress of being the breadwinner is taking its toll now that we have another child on the way. The clothes still sit in a pile – I wish they would clean themselves. I'm overwhelmed and think about how isolated everyone is these days, or maybe it's just in LA. I love to walk. I take the kids out in the double stroller, the sidewalks burning in the heat. When I'm lonely, I walk past all the little houses and wonder if we shouldn't go back to London to be around some family.

'Kevin, I want to go home. I think we should while the kids are young. It's a lot for both of us, you working all the time and me alone.'

'You really think that's a good idea? You don't really connect with your parents, your mother drives you mad. And my job is here.'

I knew he was right, but my heart craved home. No matter what, I wanted my mum right now.

* * *

I'm back in the hospital, ready to deliver. I start crying as soon as the gown is on me.

'What's wrong, dear?' the doctor asks me.

'I can't believe I'm going to have another baby. I haven't had time to think about it.'

After looking at me in disbelief he tilts his head back and roars with laughter. 'Oh, honey, you'd better believe it! This baby is on its way.'

She comes easier than her siblings. I take no painkillers, as with the others – I didn't want their little systems tainted, I wanted to be awake. But this time I don't need any help from Pitocin to keep my contractions going. This time I stand in the middle of the room and in much less time, singing at the top of my lungs, this little girl comes into world. Another beautiful baby girl… I never really imagined myself having two daughters. Two sisters. I have a biological sister who I was not raised with, but my girls will have each other. I feel strong, like centuries of women who have given birth before me.

I feel more of a connection to the human race than I have before.

I have little time to think about myself, my kids won't allow it. They say things that make me cry with laughter. I never tire of giving them hugs and kisses. I love all of them equally and deeply. I never understand it when a mother says that one child is her favourite – how can she feel that way?

'Gary,' my mother had said to me when I was a teenager, 'is just easier to love than you.' She was hurt, angry at my depressive mood and my withdrawn manner. I frustrated her and I knew it. But I also had some insight.

'Gary is easier to love because he lets you do everything for him. I don't want you involved in everything. And that's an awful thing to say to me.'

I never got used to my mother and her directness, even as I grew older – I knew it was more about her than me, yet it never failed to hurt.

* * *

We seem like the perfect family to everyone, that's what I'm told.

'Oh, your husband is so amazing! What an incredible man, a fantastic father! He loves you so much. You're so lucky.'

I do feel lucky, don't get me wrong, but I find that the

perfection that everyone sees in Kevin is getting hard to live up to. He is always so excessively nice to everyone. No matter how much I recover, I still feel moody. I gossip, bitch and complain. When I'm around him, I feel like I fail to measure up. I hear his sighs of 'here she goes again'. I see his looks of disapproval, but when I let him close he is different, more confident.

'Men get all their self-esteem from having sex,' Cassie tells me knowingly. 'It's easy. All you have to do is shag him a lot, and your life will be even more perfect.'

'Oh, really?' I say sarcastically. 'And you would know all about that, wouldn't you?'

* * *

I can't sleep. I get out of the family bed, with all three children and Kevin snoring. They look so peaceful, the way they lie tangled together.

Kevin brought me a British newspaper back from a work trip to London earlier that week and I grab it hungrily now, flicking through the pages, catching up on news of home when much to my surprise I find the advert for a detective who helps people look for family. As I stare at her details I find my eyes welling up. I never thought about my birth father much anymore; I did when I first met Pat, but my anger was so intense at her seeming lack of interest in helping me, I had to find a way to accept the situation.

But the other day, as I sat and watched my little girls play with their daddy, the way he tossed them on his shoulders, the way he smothered them with kisses, I had to admit to myself that I felt jealous. But I can never say that out loud. Who would feel jealous of their own daughters? I know I'm over the top in my parenting, trying to make sure they never feel any sense of loss or abandonment in the way that I did. I'm hopeful their beginning will free them to move forward with ease. I'm battling with the reality that my past still slows so many things down – I can't make myself go any faster in my recovery.

I'm grieving for a man I've never met, that I don't even know. I wonder if he thinks about me; I imagine he must do so sometimes. I wonder what his face looks like. My new baby daughter looks Italian – I know in my gut she looks like him.

I decide to be brave and tell Pat again that I need to meet my father, then and there, knowing the time difference back at home means she'll be awake. Many years have passed since we first met. Maybe some memories will have come back to her? I try not to cry as I speak, but I do. I put it down to hormones and being a new mother again.

'I just need to know, Pat. Sometimes I find it so hard to think that I will live my whole life never knowing.'

'I've told you everything. I'm sorry, I should have done more back then, but all I thought about was myself and getting rid of my problem – I was young, I didn't think about the future and you growing up.'

She was honest, more honest than she has ever been. The words stung, but how could I fight against the facts? She was seventeen and it was a brief fling. I was not created from two people in love, I needed to get past that. Pat was here for me now, and I was grateful for that.

So I put the phone down and contact the detective. She says it will be tough – I don't know his last name. We place an ad in an Italian newspaper anyway, but we don't receive anything back.

I wish I didn't want to know so much.

* * *

I used to go to Brighton a lot when I was younger. My grandmother's sister owned a hotel on the seafront. I loved wandering around its huge rooms. The ocean was just across the street, with a pebble beach. When I was a teenager I took friends there for Sunday lunch so we could get away from London. I liked how glamorous my grandmother's sister was, but I never felt she was really an aunt, just a familiar stranger that I knew. I'm looking out across the vast ocean in Santa Monica. The pier reminds me of those times. Kevin is running around like a lunatic and the kids are chasing him. I'm smiling, watching them. I've been feeling disconnected again and I don't like it. Sometimes

I look at the four of them as one unit, and I feel like an outsider, but then I remember that I'm their mother and I cherish each moment – I have decided that I will always be somewhere in between.

Kevin thinks I have secrets. He thinks I don't tell him everything, but why would he want to know the entire contents of my head?

I dreamt about my ex-lover last night. He was in a coffin draped in red velvet. My brother Gary was there and an old junkie that I used to buy my drugs from. I wake up wondering if this means I'm now cured, that the coffin was a sign that my old life was dead to me, but I wasn't really sure. I shudder suddenly under the hot sun.

9

London, 2005

We are heading home, back to London for a holiday. I'm so excited and the kids are too. They look so cute as they walk ahead of us towards the plane. We've taken them since they were babies so they're used to travelling but now they're older it's more fun and definitely easier. They are seated altogether, watching different movies, as I catch Kevin's eye and we smile at each other.

My mother is beaming, so happy to have us all around to fuss over – it's nice for the children too. It's unusually warm in London, which is always at its best in the sunshine.

It turns out that there's an Italian festival being held outside St Peter's Church on Clerkenwell Road. It's a ridiculously long shot, but a girl who knows I've been looking for my father emailed me the information. I want to see if anyone knows my birth father so I made flyers to hand out. Kevin was supportive and happy to come along with the kids. I put a photo of myself on them as I look now and a picture of me as a baby. It's silly, as he didn't even see me as a baby but I've got to try.

I've typed up all the information I know: he worked as a waiter in Piccadilly, he met my mum Patricia at Les Enfants Terribles and he was about twenty-two years old in 1964. A friend of mine helps me write it all out in Italian as well.

I don't tell my mother what I'm doing. The only time we ever talked about him was when I told her that I had found Pat. I felt her judgement on him, on both my birth parents for their behaviour. She won't even let me be excited about being Italian as to her somehow that denies my Jewishness. Even Pat was negative about him – 'He was good-looking, but probably from a poor fishing village.'

'Fishing village?' I asked.

'Well, he said he was from Rome, but they probably all said that.'

I'm thrilled that I'm Italian. It feels exotic to me. I hope he's a Casanova, a real charmer.

We jump on a double decker bus. The children are so excited as they had never been on one before. We get off where the streets are crowded with people, Italian accents filling the air. A live musician smiles as he plays the accordion. Kevin follows me with all the children. I notice how the Italians have badges pinned to their clothes with different coloured ribbons, representing where they were from in Italy and where they now live in England. There are booths with people selling food and a stand with flyers but I decide to take a peek in the church first – I've always loved churches and here the pews are filled to the brim. I notice a handsome man with a little boy perched on his lap, many old women dressed in black, with wrinkled faces and scarves on their heads. I stand in the doorway, watching, thinking that somewhere out there I have a biological grandmother, possibly looking just like these women. I see them line up to take their bread and wine. I've been raised Jewish, so it feels a little odd to think that this could have been my religion too.

'I can definitely get a Christmas tree without feeling guilty.' I mutter to Kevin as we walk back outside into the crowd.

I'm holding the flyers out in my hand, feeling rather awkward. *How do I start? Do I just thrust them into men's passing hands? Do I stop them?* I wonder for a second if I actually have the courage to do this. Then I spy a group of three men who look like they could be his age.

'Excuse me, sir, so sorry to bother you…' I have gone all polite and British. 'Would you look at these flyers? I'm trying to find an Italian man.'

A very tall man takes the flyer and looks with interest, reading slowly. He pauses for a moment then looks at me.

'You're trying to find an Italian man? Lucky him!'

I start blushing.

'No, not like that.' I pause and then decide to just tell the truth. He listens curiously. 'I was adopted, I'm looking for my birth father.'

Straight away, his reaction is emotional.

'Aw, you are looking for your papa. That is so very sad.'

I smile, unsure how to respond. He starts yelling to the men he has been with, who have wandered away.

'Mario, Franco, come back here! This lady, she is looking for her father.'

I'm immediately surrounded by all three, showing the flyer to one another.

'We all went to this club, Les Enfants Terribles. It was wonderful – we had drinks, we danced, we met the ladies,' the first man says to me.

'We always came in pairs,' adds a shorter man with a very thick accent. 'Someone here knows him, I guarantee. We're going to help you.'

They ask me more questions about my life, my adoption.

'You look Italian.' The tall man pinches my cheeks. 'You are a lovely lady.'

'Thank you.'

They have taken a few flyers and the tall man has my

phone number – he promises to let me know if he has any news. He talks to a lady at a booth, who looks up at me and takes a flyer. She says I should go and talk to the priest.

I find Kevin standing in the shade with the kids. They all have ice cream and seem content. I explain what I was doing but it's hard for them to really understand. As we head back towards the church, I spy a man leaning against the fence all by himself; he is dressed in a lovely suit, a silk scarf around his neck. We catch each other's eye and he smiles at me.

'Wait here just a minute,' I tell Kevin and the kids.

'Excuse me, sir, would you mind reading my flyer? I was adopted and I'm searching for my father.' I decide to say it straight away, as it seems to get people more interested. He reads it slowly, then looks up at me.

'My name is Antonio.' The blood rushes to my head. 'But,' he pauses, 'I did not come to London until 1967, so too late for it to be me. And I'm rather short.'

We laugh. He is very good-looking – I wouldn't have minded if he were my father.

'My wife of many years died just a few months ago.' His eyes are full of tears.

'I'm so sorry for your loss,' I tell him.

He looks me directly in the eye.

'I wish it were me, I wish it were true. I would be very proud to be your father.'

I'm completely taken aback by his words and my eyes fill like his.

'Are those your children?'

We both look over at the kids and Kevin.

'Yes,' I say proudly.

'Oh!' he sighs. 'So beautiful. Your father, he is missing so much.'

I bribe the kids with fizzy drinks, saying that I just need to pop in and talk to the priest. They don't know what a priest is, but they're thrilled – I never give them fizzy drinks normally. I'm led into a small, round room. The priest is a heavyset man, encased in his robes and seated behind a large dark wooden table. He is very high up in the Italian Church, I was told, a very kind and helpful man.

I sit opposite him, feeling small and shy.

'How can I help you?' His voice is full and loud.

'I was adopted. I know my father is Italian and his name is Antonio.' I feel silly saying it out loud, and then a wave of shame comes over me for not knowing more.

He is serious and calm.

'Do you know his last name?'

'No, I don't.' I'm sinking in my seat, hating how many times I have had to tell people my truth. He looks thoughtful but doesn't say anything.

What I really want to say is, *No, I don't know his name. My mother was young and she fucked a man she barely knew.*

We've all behaved like that at some point in our lives, haven't we? So, Mr Priest, I'm not pure at all. I came into this world shameful, a secret. So that makes me bad. I know that's what you're thinking.

But I don't, of course. We both stay quiet for a moment as I see him considering the situation.

'I'm sorry, I really do not know how I can help.'

'May I give you my flyers?' I ask, disappointed.

He shakes his head. 'No, I have nowhere to put them. I suggest the community centre downstairs.'

I come back into the daylight, cloaked with melancholy. *He wasn't that kind*, I think to myself, *or compassionate*. I kiss the children, wondering how many other women like me have visited the priest with a similar story.

* * *

'Zara,' she told me on the phone tearfully, 'I may as well just let myself die. They want me on dialysis and I can't do that – there's no going back. I just want to die, I've had enough.'

I'm cautious, unsure of what to say.

'Mum, we want you alive as long as possible, but obviously, it's your choice. I know it will be hard, but please think about it.'

She has decided to give it a go. On Monday, Wednesday and Friday she will go and sit for three hours on a machine while they filter her blood. She has adapted as best she can, watching movies and reading to pass the time. She always arrives in a nice dress and lipstick.

'There's an old lady there,' my mother tells me proudly, 'who tells me that she likes to see what I'm wearing when I come in. She says I always look so lovely.'

I laugh out loud and tell her how much I admire her for making such an effort.

We always seem to get along better when she is vulnerable and sick, I think to myself as I close the door to my brother's old bedroom. I lie down on his small bed. The room has been repainted since he lived here, but to me it still has a tinge of the old energy. Even paint wasn't able to eradicate that altogether. I feel a pang of longing for the children, but I knew it was easier for me to come alone: Mum doesn't have the same energy that she used to. She is suffering with a raw red rash all over her body. I had applied cream earlier to try and help ease the itching – I don't like seeing her this way.

I turn off the light and try to sleep, but the memories are flooding my mind. They do whenever I'm back in this house. But this one is something I thought I'd forgotten. I had never talked about this to anyone.

It's 1981. My mum and dad have just left the house. I wait patiently as they pack up the car. I know not to start smoking the moment they leave because they always forget something so I wait ten minutes after they leave and sure enough, they are back, my mother running into the house before running out to the car again. Then I know they are gone for the weekend.

Out come the cigarettes and the pot. I roll myself a joint, turn up the music and dance around my bedroom. The freedom I feel when they're not around me is always liberating.

The phone rings: it's my girlfriend, Mimi.

'Can I bring Adam to stay at your place tonight?'

'Yes, that's fine, but can you not be kissing in front of me?' my seventeen-year-old self says.

They go to their room pretty quickly after they arrive, desperate to be alone. I don't mind – I'm just glad to know they're in the house with me. I love my parents being away but I still get scared on my own. I must have fallen asleep eventually, as I'm woken with a jump. The light from the hallway is bright and my book has fallen to the floor. I look at the clock: it's 3am and my brother is back with some friends.

The Grateful Dead has been turned on at full volume. I can hear some muffled talking. I'm so angry; this happens a lot. I lie for at least an hour, trying to fall asleep but the music is so loud, it's impossible. I pluck up the courage and walk sleepily into his room, opening the door to a couple of familiar faces. I know in an instant that my brother is out of it – I've been gauging his moods for years.

'Gary, it's past 3am. Turn the music down, please – I was asleep. Turn it down.' I hear the pleading in my voice.

He sneers at me from his bed, his friends on the floor next to him: 'You are such a selfish bitch! I have people over.'

'It's the middle of the night,' I try to reason, 'how can you say I'm selfish? Turn it down.'

I leave the room quickly and go back to lie on my bed, my fear rising. I hear him coming, my body aware of his presence before my mind. My door is swung open. He grabs me, both hands around my neck, his face contorted with rage. His large body moves in and out of the shadows, the light from the corridor spilling into my room.

'Have I told you how sick I am of you?' he begins. 'You are the most selfish bitch and cunt that I've ever met.' He's pulling me up and down by my neck as he spits words of venom into my face. My head is being pushed down into my pillow. 'You are a slag, a slut. That's what you are, nothing but a bastard, a total bastard. I have people over!' His yelling is louder, his hands grow tighter about my neck. 'Your mother didn't want you, because you're so selfish. It's no surprise she gave you away.'

His hands are still holding my neck – he won't stop pulling me up and down. I try to yell out, but I can't move my mouth. I try to fight, but I'm too weak. Up and down, up and down, until I'm sure my neck will break. I can feel myself going dizzy, his face now blurred. I can't make out his words. Was he truly going to kill me and end up in prison for the rest of his life? *Does he realise that I can't breathe, can't he tell that he needs to stop?* Then I hear Adam coming up behind my brother, wrestling with him. He tries for a moment to unlock Gary's hands. I hear him yell; I try to open my eyes.

'Stop, you have to stop!'

But my brother holds on tight. Adam is still yelling. I can feel his hands as he tries to pry Gary off me. When I feel a sudden release, I choke in a big gasp of air. I fall back onto the bed. My heart beats rapidly, the oxygen flowing back into my body. My brother has left, laughing at Adam.

Adam peers at me from the shadows, his eyes full of concern: 'Are you okay?'

I feel myself nod automatically. That's what I always did – I said I was okay even when I wasn't. My insides are shaken with terror.

'Are you sure?' He looks at me kindly for a moment but we know that this situation is way too big for either of us.

I don't cry that night – I think I'm in too much shock – but I feel a wrap go around my heart in a way that it never has before. I feel myself sink deeper and deeper, further away from everyone.

10

St John's Wood, London, July 24th 2008

I will always remember how the light changed that early summer evening from a soft grey to the deepest black, as I sat looking at my mother in her hospital bed. A hush had fallen over the room. The nurses had left us alone to say goodbye. I held my mother's hand during those final moments, a panic in my chest as I felt her leave, those soft hands that had nurtured me in the best way she knew how. My father sat on the other side of her, staring at the ground and muttering words that I couldn't make out.

It was the summer following my last visit. I knew my mother was unwell and we were all planning to go to London again. A vast distance had invaded my marriage. We had recently moved to New Jersey due to my husband being laid off, finally leaving LA behind. I had cried a lot while saying goodbye to everyone there. I had told Kevin that I was willing to give it a go for him, but asked if we could move back to London if it didn't work out.

'You've never lived in another part of the States,' he had said, 'I think you'll like it.'

The truth is I was scared. I had moved countries once and it had taken so long to find people with whom I felt a connection. And now that I had, we were leaving again. I loved New York, but when we got there Kevin's job fell through. He fell apart, feeling guilty for moving his family into an unstable situation. I had become close with a man that I had met at my support group, another adoptee. The friendship threw me. Kevin was jealous and I couldn't explain the connection I was feeling.

'It's a feeling of familiarity,' my therapist had reassured me on the phone. 'It can feel like more, but it isn't. It often happens to adopted people when they meet.'

But it had shaken me. I had never stepped outside my marriage before. I had never had feelings towards another man. I felt understood, but I also knew that I had cracked the door open and let the stranger in, even if it was only for a few moments.

Instead of coming together, Kevin and I started to fight. It was a combination of all the stress of moving, and for me the thought of losing my mother. But we all flew to London for a family holiday.

My mother is not well. I'm taken aback when we get there as she looks so frail and she hasn't told me how bad she is. She can barely breathe and before our visit ends she is admitted to hospital for another bypass surgery.

'I need to stay,' I tell Kevin, 'and help her. Take the kids back home.'

'Can you stay and look after Dad?' she asked before the surgery.

'Yes Mum, of course – and you too.' She cried as I spoke, she was so grateful I was staying. 'Just let me get the kids home. From Thursday morning you'll have all my attention.'

But she couldn't wait until Thursday: she passed away at 5.30pm on the Wednesday, just as Kevin and the kids were boarding the plane.

I had loved my mother. I had needed my mother, although at times I couldn't bear to be in the same room as her. She consumed me, watching, always I felt, with such a critical eye, suffocating my every move. I had spent years pushing her away and pulling her back to me. She was kind, there was no doubt, and I knew she loved me. I had been so afraid of her rejection that I went to great lengths to make sure it would never happen. But it was complicated. I never felt free to be myself with her, I couldn't explore my opinions the way a child does – it was not allowed. As a young child I had pretended to friends, neighbours, my grandparents, that everything was all right in our family. I had to prove to them that we were the same as everyone else, or at least how my mother perceived others. She did not want anyone knowing about our arguments. It made her feel ashamed, as if it were a reflection on her as a mother. However, I struggled with this falsehood. I never felt the same as anyone around me. My family didn't look like me and I was often questioned about it – 'Why does your mother have blonde hair and you don't?', 'Why are you so skinny?', 'How come your mother has boobs when you've got nothing much going on?', 'Why don't you look like your mother?'

If anyone said those things in front of her, she would respond, 'She looks just like her father.'

Angry, I stayed quiet as she lied. Why couldn't she just tell everyone the truth? Why was it a secret? The four of us had come together in very different circumstances from those of my friends' families. I wanted them to know I wasn't ashamed yet the layers of grief hidden within each of us made it impossible to speak the truth. My parents had to cope with their unresolved loss, their childlessness. My brother and I, born of different mothers, carried within us the unseen wounds of our birth mothers' abandonment. My adoptive mother didn't want me to tell anyone the big secret; she was ashamed. And the worst part for her was the lie all those people told her, that adopting us would heal her barrenness, that she would feel like a real fertile mother once she held us in her arms. And that all we needed was to be loved. I don't believe she ever did. She had been a kind woman, no doubt about that. She relished the chance to be a mother, but she could never talk about our situation, or how we felt.

In that moment that I lost her, I knew that she and I had been meant to be together. Maybe it was for a cosmic reason, part of the grand master plan that none of us would ever truly understand. It had taken me so many years to let her in, and I felt so much sorrow for both of us over those wasted years. As I held her hand, I no longer blamed her or even myself: I blamed circumstance. As I sat by her side, I heard her say softly, her eyes still closed, 'I can't do this anymore.' Then I knew that the years of illness had finally won: she could no longer will herself to stay with us.

I lean towards her and whisper back, 'It's okay, Mum, you don't have to – I'll take care of Dad and Gary for you.'

I watch her body visibly relax and sink slightly into the bed. She has stopped breathing. Her mouth is half-open, a trace of blood visible on her tongue. Only a lingering resistance is left on her face as she enters the next world.

I stay for a while longer, still holding her hand. I twist her ring around that familiar, comforting hand the same way I had done as a child. I didn't want them to take my mother away, I wasn't ready to leave her. But as the night grew later and darker, I knew there would never be a right moment to leave. *They would have to tear me away from her*, I thought.

The Jewish undertaker arrives. I'm only wearing a tank top and my arms are bare so he doesn't look directly at me.

'You must take all her jewellery off, no rings.' He glances at my mother's hand.

'She can't wear her wedding ring?'

'No jewellery.'

I lift up my mother's hand. It has become cold so quickly, and so stiff. I'm trying to pull off the ring, but her fingers are so swollen it seems impossible.

'Please,' the man offers.

I watch as he tries to twist and turn the ring, but it won't budge.

'I will go and get my implement. Excuse me.' He shuffles out of the room.

Is he about to cut off her finger?

I lift her hand again, the thought now worrying me. I pull. Still nothing. *Oh shit*, I think. Then her voice in my ear, so loud it cuts through every other thought in my head.

'Oh, for goodness' sake, Zara! Give it a jolly good pull.'
So I do, and suddenly it has slid off. I'm holding it as the undertaker walks back in, surprise on both our faces.

My father has his coat on, keys in his hand. He's chewing his stubby nails the way he has always done. I pick up my mother's handbag, keeping my eyes on her as I leave the room until the curtain is pulled shut, hiding her completely. We drive home from the hospital in silence.

As I get into bed that night, I pick up the cardigan she has left on her chair. Holding it to my face, I inhale her smell as deeply as I can, for I know in time it will fade. I wrap it around me. All night I can smell her perfume. It comforts me. I lie awake for a long time, staring into the darkness. How can it be possible? My mother, who had survived so many illnesses, had finally succumbed. Like a little child I had believed that she could survive anything. If anyone could come back from the dead, it would be her. Because if she couldn't come back, I wasn't quite sure how any of us were going to manage.

Finally I fall into a restless sleep. It was the start of weeks of unsettling dreams, in which I saw my mother lying in her hospital bed, taking her last breath.

* * *

The funeral is two days later, as is the Jewish tradition. Pat had asked if she could attend, but I declined. My two mothers had never met and even after all these years it was hard for Mum. I didn't feel that I could ask my dad – they hadn't even wanted Pat at my wedding.

For years I have lived with this double family – a split life, never fully resolved. I don't know anymore how to bring them together. As the week goes by I find that I'm avoiding talking to Pat. She keeps reaching out to me but I don't want to be in contact right now – I can't talk to her about the grief I'm feeling. I'm consumed by a fierce loyalty towards my mother. I don't know how to explain it; I don't want to hurt her.

Our last holiday as a family had been to the Gambia when I was fifteen. I wondered why was I suddenly thinking about this as I stood listening to the rabbi saying the prayers. My eyes are full of tears that won't fall. I'm transfixed by the candles: as their flames burn higher and brighter, I'm convinced my mother is talking to me through them.

Cassie looks at me from across the room. I manage a slight smile. She has tears in her eyes. She has known my mother her whole life – she had loved her too.

My mother's family and friends stand all around the room, old Jewish men and women so small, I tower over them. I see the teachers from the school where she volunteered, the priest from the school, the Conservative Party members. They've all come to pay their respects. She had led a full life and committed herself to many causes. I feel proud of her. She had never given up her passions, no matter how sick she became.

I listen as they pray, their bodies swaying. *How many Shivas have they been to by now*, I wonder. The flames from the candles dance, conjuring an image of our family.

I'm usually silent when I'm with my family. I'm as quiet

as possible, headphones in my ears to drown out their voices and lose myself. I didn't really know what to expect from Africa, but I was excited to see a beautiful hotel, huts scattered all around, surrounded by the whitest sand I had ever seen. It seemed to go on endlessly. Within hours, we're on the beach. My brother has already run off into the ocean.

I lie on my back, feeling the warm sand beneath me. I drift in and out of sleep. I'm surprised by some young men standing close by, looking down at me. Their teeth look so white against their beautiful black skin – I had never known skin so dark.

'What is your name?' one young boy asks, surprisingly well. 'You English?'

'Zara,' I reply, nodding. I realise that my mother has joined my brother in the ocean and my father has disappeared.

'That your mother?'

They point in her direction.

'Yes,' I reply.

They sit next to me without waiting for an invitation. Then they tell me they work at the hotel as busboys and kitchen staff. I feel cautious, wondering what they want.

'You smoke?' the same guy asks. He offers me a cigarette but I decline, pointing to my mother. They laugh.

'Later, you come to the kitchen, you hide with us and smoke.'

I smile.

'Maybe I will,' I tell them.

'How old are you?'

'Fifteen,' I say, sitting up straight.

The other guys stand to leave, but my new friend stays.

'What's your name?' I ask.

'Robbie,' he answers. I can see small beads of sweat glimmering on his forehead.

'That's not an African name,' I observe, looking into his dark eyes.

His mouth widens into a beautiful grin. 'Easier for you English to say.' He stands up, offering me his hand to shake. 'Come to the kitchen later, we not bite.'

My mother comes ambling back. 'Who were those boys?' she asks vaguely.

'Hotel staff,' I reply dismissively.

'Come into the water with me, Zara, it's so warm,' she tells me.

I nod and my mother smiles; we walk along the white sand, into the sparkling ocean. For a little while, we are able to relax with one another.

I didn't go to the kitchen that evening – my mother wouldn't allow it. We all went to bed very early. My brother and I are sharing a room. I try to sleep as he spits nasty comments in my direction.

'Didn't know you liked darkies, Zara,' he whispers in the dark. I don't respond. 'Well, I suppose there are a lot to choose from here. As for me I'm going to get high as a kite. Best weed in the world, you know.'

I still don't speak, hoping he'll think I'm asleep.

* * *

It's three days until I can finally go and see the boys in the kitchen. My parents want a date night, which is fine with me. I promise them I will stay close by. I had seen Robbie each day – we would wave and smile to each other. Sometimes I could see him watching me from across the terrace as we ate breakfast outside. As I walk into the kitchen, I smell the sweetness of the spices and a huge cooking pot full of rice and vegetables.

Robbie comes towards me immediately. He takes my hand and introduces me to all the staff. Everyone is so welcoming. Helping carry a big bowl of rice, we walk outside into a small hut, where some other workers are already sitting a low table. Robbie shows me how they eat with their hands. I watch for a moment before joining in. We all eat from the same bowl.

'Your family,' he says between mouthfuls, 'are you sure they're your family?'

I laugh with surprise.

'Of course they're my family. I wouldn't just show up with strangers, would I?' I say.

He shakes his head.

'No, but you don't look like your mother or father. You don't act like them, either – you're different.'

At this I'm silent, focusing on the bowl in front of me. I feel his gaze on me. 'You seem like a sad girl. I was watching you and your family. They are not the same as you and your brother – I don't like him.'

'How can you tell?' I whisper.

'It is easy to tell,' he replies confidently. 'I heard him the other morning. He talks to you with venom on his tongue. Why would he be so unkind?'

'He can't help himself,' I say, quickly defending him.

'Everyone can help themselves if they want to,' he replies kindly.

'I used to believe that, Robbie. I don't anymore.'

I begin to cry softly, tears running down my face. I brush them away quickly so he won't see, but the more I try, the faster they come.

Robbie sits beside me on the dusty floor, his arm around my shoulder. I lean into him, my chest now heaving. I feel like my tears will never stop.

'They are my family, but they aren't,' I say between gasps. 'I love my mother and I know she loves me, but I have another one, you see. Another mother and father somewhere out there. I don't know who they are, or what they do, or why my mother couldn't raise me.'

'You are a strong girl,' Robbie whispers reassuringly. 'You

can leave this family one day and make your own life. You will be okay.' He takes my face in his hands, gently wiping away my tears. I manage to smile at him.

I spend the rest of the week with Robbie and his friends, ignoring the taunts of my brother. 'Oh, you're going to get in trouble,' he says cruelly, between bites of watermelon.

'Don't be getting pregnant with no darkie baby.'

On the last day, I'm filled with such dread of leaving. I had never felt so safe with anyone before Robbie. When he comes to say goodbye, wrapping his arms around me in a tight hug, he pushes into my hand a little wooden carving of a man's face.

'Who is that?' I'm looking at the piece, touching its face with my thumb.

'He very wise, he will bring you luck. Keep it always, Miss Zara.'

'Robbie,' I feel awkward, 'how come you never tried to kiss me? My brother said that was all you really wanted. Do you not like me?'

He looks down at me with his beautiful deep brown eyes. His brow furrows. 'Oh, Miss, I think about it all the time. But don't give away those kisses too easily,' he tells me. And he kisses me gently on the mouth, his lips soft and full.

We write to each other for a few years after that. He tells me in one letter that his girlfriend is pregnant. He says he's going to call the baby Zara, after me. I still think about this African baby, my namesake.

* * *

I haven't spoken to my brother since my mother's death. When I see him at her funeral, I can tell he's high. He is battling with cancer, his head is bald from the chemo. I know this is a very rough time for him. I catch his eye for a second, but his face gives nothing away. I know he's as lost as me right now.

At the hospital on the day she passed, we had been asked to move our cars because we might get a ticket.

'Seriously?' I had said to the nurse.

That's when the rage came. I can't even remember what started it. I was standing outside in the car park, and he was in his car. He had started screaming at me, telling me how selfish I was, that talking about my adoption had devastated our mother.

It was my turn now, and I began to spew years of pain out towards him. I was taken aback by the sheer force of it.

'You think you're so perfect? You think you did everything right?'

'You're a selfish cunt, you always have been. It's always about you,' he said, his voice louder than mine. I knew I had to stop arguing with him. What was the point? Here I was again, feeling the familiar frustration I had felt my whole life. This was a reminder of why I had moved away yet I still felt ashamed. *Was he right?* I had wanted to heal myself. *Had it worked?* I knew in my heart that I couldn't stifle myself anymore, regardless of his reaction. Gary started his engine, still shouting out the window. I said nothing more. He yelled that he was going to feed his new puppy and would be back soon.

But Mum hadn't waited for him to come back. I called to let him know that she's dying, but he didn't make it back in time. I couldn't believe that she had passed away while he was gone. I make sure they leave her body so he can say goodbye to her – I knew he needed to. When he returns, I step outside to give him his privacy. I don't want to fight anymore. I can hear him quietly talking to her, saying his goodbyes. I feel the tears slide down my face.

* * *

The prayers end. My aunt begins pouring tea and passing the cake around. I'm suddenly hungry; I haven't eaten all day. Sitting on a low mourner's chair, I allow them to wait on me, grateful for traditions that evening.

'Do you think Mum would feel it was weird for me to eat right now?' I ask my aunt.

'Your mother think it weird?' She cackles loudly 'Your mother ate her way through everything in her life. When she was happy, she ate, when she was sad, she ate. She would be delighted. Now eat some cake.' Her eyes are gentle. 'My dear, I know you had your differences, but your mother loved you very much. She was so proud of you. You do know that, don't you?'

Nodding without speaking, I feel my heart break. I know that I will never be quite the same again.

I stay with my father for another two weeks. Standing in the kitchen one afternoon, I look at this now vulnerable man. I flash back to a time when I stood in that very same spot as a teenager. I had been half-hidden behind the door to escape the way he looked at me. He would stare quietly, his eyes locked on mine, no smile on his face. I knew that he understood what he meant by this silent transaction. I had told him I didn't like it, but to him it seemed like a game. I felt controlled. His only words were, 'I can look at you if I want, you're my daughter.'

And yet he had no memory of it at all. What my father never understood was how that look changed me, how his constant silence broke me in ways that took years to repair. For the last two weeks we had been together, we talked in a way we never had before.

Regardless of how he has been in the past, I still cry as I finally say goodbye to my father, watching him wave as I get in the cab to the airport. He had appeared so big when I was a child but now he looks so small, so sad. My grief was allowing my heart to soften towards him in spite of everything. I was feeling less angry.

There's no doubt that people come together after a death. Grief can crumble the highest and hardest walls.

* * *

A few months before my mother passed away Pat asked me if she could talk to her. She had always wanted to meet her but my mother had never really been able to do that so I had never pushed it. To my surprise she finally agreed, and once they got off the phone both of them called me at the same time.

'So I spoke to Pat, she was very nice,' my mother said.

'Yes Mum, she is nice', I answered.

'She was so, so well. You know… she didn't sound… as I had thought.' My mum is stumbling on her words.

'You mean she doesn't sound as educated as you, as posh?'

I knew my Mum well enough to know what she was getting at.

'Well, yes.' And I could hear the relief in her voice. It clearly comforted her.

That night I dreamt I was sitting on a sofa in between both my mother's, my purse was open and all my cards were scattered on the sofa and the floor as I was desperately trying to find my driving licence, my identity.

A week before my mum died she called and asked where

Somebody's Daughter

I was and I told her I was with Pat, not hiding it from her as I might have done in the past. My mum simply said 'say hello from me'. And as I hung up I realised that after twenty years of reunion my mum was finally able to give me her blessing to have a relationship, and I felt this incredible weight fall from me. Now that my mum was gone, I didn't have to feel bad or guilty. I had closure.

11

New York, 2008

'What's wrong with you?' my husband says with frustration a couple of weeks after my return. I had pushed him out of the bedroom again.

'I want her to come back, I just want her to come back,' I cry like a child. My sadness is engulfing me. An old panic has settled in, the one I lived with as a child when my adoptive mother ever ventured away. I'm having the same feeling of separation anxiety. How could that be? I was an adult; this was ridiculous.

'Are you going to let me back in? Tell me what's going on,' Kevin asks stiffly. 'It's endless, it's too much. You're an adult. When is this going to stop? You have to move on, Zara – people die all the time. I know she was your mother,

159

but you're not a child.' He reaches out to hug me and I find myself stiffening at his touch. It confuses me. It has surprised me also, the depth of emotion I have reached: he's right, it's too much.

'It's not my fault,' I scream at him. 'Do you think anyone wants to feel this way? But I keep seeing her dying over and over.'

'You have to try and stop going there, focus on the children.' He's trying, but he's frustrated with me and I can't blame him. My mother used to feel the same way.

But I can't stop myself from sinking and isolating myself. I'm lost in grief. I hug her memory to me. All I know is not to drink or take a drug. I'm trying to do normal things, but I have no focus. Everything feels different now my mother has gone. Kevin and I have stopped laughing together; we bicker all the time. It is not fun for any of us. And then there was Simon.

He was a band photographer I had met when I first became a backing singer, many years ago. I had fallen for him so easily. I'd looked up to him. He made me laugh and he taught me things about art and photography. The chemistry between us consumed me. When I became sober, I moved away from that crowd. I knew that I felt a weakness around him. I was never going to be his girlfriend, that much was apparent. I also knew that if one day I wanted to have a family of my own, I needed to stay away. Yet I'd thought about him over the years, hearing snippets about his life.

A mutual friend contacted me, saying she had bumped into him. I asked her to give him my number and he called. He made me laugh the moment we spoke. He seemed happy, he was in a long-term relationship. We begin to text, sporadically at first. We make plans that the next time I was in London we would meet for coffee. I'm cautious, but enjoying the flirtation. It stops me focusing on what I need to do.

'Who are you texting?' my husband asks suspiciously as I walk into the bedroom.

'Cassie,' I lie, too quickly.

Kevin wants to hold me the moment I lay on the bed. He needs reassurance, but I can't seem to give him any. I manage for a moment to relax into his arms. Taking that as me wanting more, he begins to kiss me slowly. I respond for a brief moment before pulling away, unable to bear the look of sadness on my husband's face. He rolls over silently and falls asleep. I lie in the dark hating myself, until sleep takes over.

I dream that my mother is standing on a beach with the whitest sand, just like in Africa. Her hair is blowing in the breeze, the ocean behind her. She is wearing a white nightdress and she looks young again. I stand opposite her and I begin to cry, tears trickling down my face.

Somebody's Daughter

Taking my hand, she whispers to me, but I can barely hear her over the roar of the ocean. She leads me along the beach to a small hut, where some people have gathered outside. As we walk past, I see them looking at me, but I don't recognise anyone. She points to a small door. As I open it, she says, 'This is your father, and these ladies are his sisters, your aunts. They want so much to meet you.'

It dawns on me what she really means. Stepping into the doorway I see the shadow of a man. I'm exhilarated. He starts to turn his face towards me, but then the darkness envelopes us. Realising I'm alone, I walk slowly towards him. My eyes now strain in the dark, searching. I want to see his face, just a glimpse, but the shadows will not leave him. I must have been talking in my sleep.

Sitting bolt upright in bed, I turn to my husband in the dark and wake him up.

'I need to find my father to complete my circle. Meeting my mother just wasn't enough. I know my life will change if I can just meet him. Every night since Mum died, I dream about her one night and him the next. And now both of them together. I don't understand it, I haven't thought about him for ages. Maybe it's a sign?'

I feel my husband lie back down.

'You said that about meeting your mother, you thought that might fix you too. And I'm sure in some ways it did, but you say you don't always feel fully part of her family because too many years went by. It's not about meeting your parents, it's about accepting that you have parents you didn't grow up with. Maybe finding him will help, but it isn't the whole answer,' he tells me.

'How can you say that, after you've learnt so much about adoption and helped me with this? You know meeting Pat made a tremendous difference to my life. I know it's hard for people to understand. I haven't forgotten your kindness and your patience. It's not been easy, but look at what I've learnt about myself.'

Touching his back gently for the first time in a long while, I let out a heavy sigh. Now it's him who pulls away.

'What did you learn? Did you learn how to love me? I don't think you did.' His voice is full of hurt. He can no longer contain his resentment. 'It's still all about you, isn't it? It always has been.'

'You know, the way you go on is so unattractive. You always blame me for everything, like it's my fault I have these unknown parents,' I reply, feeling the anger. 'It doesn't make me want to fuck you, if that's what you're getting at.'

'Zara,' he says sharply, 'it's not the way I act that makes you not want to have sex with me. It's because knowing you, you're probably flirting with someone else. You don't know how to maintain intimacy.' He turns away from me. 'I need to sleep. Do what you want, but don't expect me to keep supporting you. I don't have the energy anymore.'

Somebody's Daughter

I'm silent, his words left stinging in the air. 'How are we going to fix this?' I murmur. But he doesn't respond.

'It takes two people to fix a marriage,' a therapist had told us months before. My husband had agreed that he wanted to work things out, that I was the one for him. I knew, though, years ago he had been maintaining a very close relationship with his new boss, although he denied it. I couldn't blame him – he was a man that needed attention and he wasn't getting it from me. I found it irritating anyway.

'I mean, really? You're fucking your boss? You're so obvious.' I had confronted him after our third child was born, exhausted from being home alone all day. I felt unattractive. Like most mothers at that stage, I believed I would never be back to my normal self.

'I am not having an affair with my boss,' he stated again and again.

'But why do you talk about her all the time? I'm so sick of hearing about her – Lisa this and Lisa that. It's fucking weird, she's your boss.'

But he had denied anything else was going on.

'It's my fault,' I said to my girlfriend while I nursed my little one. 'I've been so exhausted with these babies I haven't wanted sex with him.' I pause for a moment. 'To be honest, I haven't wanted sex with him because I don't feel connected to him anymore. I'm never good enough for him, but I'm going to try and be more accepting.'

Therapy didn't work. I knew I didn't feel the same way as him. I wanted to, but I couldn't seem to muster up the feelings: I had lost the will to make it work. We had both become so critical of each other, taking every word as hateful. It was as though we were speaking in different languages.

'You call yourself a therapist?' I said in anger one afternoon. Nothing had changed in my marriage. She had just nodded, smiling at me in that superior way. 'What makes you think you can help us? Are you married?'

'Well, I've been doing this for twenty years and had a lot of successes,' she answers, her manicured hands are folded in her lap.

'I need to ask you a question…' I continue. I feel my husband stiffen. 'Is therapy supposed to help you accept yourself? Does it allow you to make changes?'

She nods smugly. *How much money did she make from this? Three hundred dollars for two people, for fifty minutes.* I start calculating her day's wages, feeling my anger rise.

'We've come to you three times already, and all you do is ask us how we feel. We've told you how we feel, over and over. And then you have the nerve to tell me to hug him? I don't want to hug him, do you understand? I've told you that he demands it at home. It's not natural to be told when to show affection, even I know that. And now you tell me I have to hug him here, in your office. Well, I don't want to.'

Somebody's Daughter

I stand up and put on my coat. Kevin follows me to the car.

'Why has she had so much Botox on her face? I can't read her expression. Maybe she should go to therapy and figure out why ageing terrifies her so much. Stupid marriage counselling!'

I stumble out of the office as if I'm drunk, laughing out loud. This was not like me; the guilt was beginning to rise. Maybe Kevin was right. Maybe I really did have irreparable issues. I wasn't sure what to believe anymore.

I decided I couldn't be that woman anymore. I was going to step back into my past, right or wrong. No matter how much I told myself that I was just going to meet up for old times' sake, I was as powerless over Simon as I had been the day we first met. My mother had been right: time had softened the raw edges of my memories, leaving only the good times. It had been a long time since I had done anything like this.

After I'd met Kevin and had my beautiful babies, I felt healed in a way I had never known before. I believed nothing could ever touch me again. Yet here I was, years later, standing at the doorway, about to cross back into my past.

Simon had been married while I was seeing him all those years ago. I was so young I didn't understand what it meant to be involved in such betrayal – I was caught up in the excitement of the secret looks, holding hands under the table. Was I willing to start all that again? It had taken so much strength of character for me to walk away the first time, almost as hard as giving up drugs.

Wake up, Zara, I tell myself. *You're married to a decent man, you can still make it work. You have three beautiful children.* My inner monologue wouldn't stop. *Would you sacrifice all of that just to prove that a man still finds you attractive? Go back, and make your marriage work.*

But I no longer knew how. It seemed impossible to bridge the gap between us. A fierce pull had taken hold of me; I needed to reconnect with my past.

12

London, 2011

My mum has been gone for a few years but I miss her so much. For the first year, I felt totally anchorless. It makes no sense: when she was alive I couldn't bear being around her, and now that she's gone all I want is to be near her again.

I'm trying to be more present. I want to make my marriage work. We're having moments of connection, but the huge gulf between us still hasn't been filled. I can't seem to get over my mother's death, and Kevin can't handle my emotions. I do what I do best when I'm in pain: I push him away. I don't want him, or anyone else to be close to me. The going back and forth between countries is taking its toll. I'm torn between wanting to return to England and doing the best for my children.

Somebody's Daughter

It has taken a few years for him to convince me but I finally agree to meet Simon while I'm back in London packing up my father's house. We are selling our family home that we have had for forty-six years – it was time to get my dad into assisted living. I can't imagine not having the home anymore and I know I'm not thinking properly.

I stand in front of the mirror, trying to decide what to wear. It's been many years since he last saw me and I want to look good. I pull on a pair of tight jeans and a black top, casual but a little bit sexy too.

'I know it's pathetic,' I tell Cassie, 'but I just want to know if he still wants me.'

'Wanting to have sex with you and wanting you are two different things. I doubt very much that he's changed. You haven't aged too badly. He's probably half-blind by now anyway, so it doesn't really matter,' she says with a cheeky smile.

'Hilarious,' I answer.

* * *

The sun shines weakly through the clouds as I drive towards Baker Street, nervous but excited. The last time he saw me I was so young. *Now I'm a mother, a middle-aged woman*, I think to myself.

I knock on the door of his office. A young man opens it. 'Yes,' he says sharply. I can hear the self-importance in his voice and I'm suddenly reminded of how people behave around Simon: they get intimidated by his presence.

I hear his voice before I see him. Then he comes running to the top of the stairs and leans over the balcony. His hair shorter than I remember, but still falls in his face the way it always did. We both smile as I climb up the stairs. He takes me in his strong arms.

'Let me look at you.' He steps back. 'You look amazing! I was worried you'd be fat after having three kids.'

Cassie was right: he hasn't changed. 'Charming,' I reply. 'You look great too, for an old man.'

I sit beside him on the sofa; I squeeze into the corner, not wanting to touch him. We eye each other cautiously. *It's always so strange, seeing someone after so many years*, I think. I'm not sure what to say, but he's good at small talk. He asks to see photos of my kids. I sense his surprise at seeing them all there in front of him. He asks me polite questions and I answer automatically, thinking about the time I had with him years ago. I still find him attractive. He's older, but still childlike. I had forgotten what an ego he has, how he doesn't care what other people think; I had always admired how free he seemed.

An hour goes by quickly. I see him looking at me and wonder what he's thinking. He's still with his girlfriend of many years; they have no children. I could never have given that up, not even for him.

He wants to spend more time with me; he asks me to drive him to his next appointment.

We walk down the street but I can't seem to find my car.

'Oh, Zara! You haven't changed, have you?' He chuckles.

'It's a rental, I just don't recognise it.' I'm embarrassed.

I feel a wave of relief as I finally spot the car. The moment we get in, he pulls me towards him and starts kissing me. For a moment I kiss him back, but then I pull away, confused and annoyed.

'I haven't seen you in all these years and you kiss me straight away, without asking?'

'Sorry, do I need to sign a contract?' He giggles sheepishly but I'm not amused.

'I haven't seen you in years.'

I'm flustered. Now that I'm with him, it's as if no time has passed at all. We're picking up right where we left off, but this time I'm not a young girl with no voice.

'You always liked my outsides, but that's about all. What about who I am on the inside? Does that still not matter to you?'

'For fuck's sake, Zara!' He rolls his eyes. 'I always knew you liked me, but I was unavailable at the time. You knew that, I never lied to you. I still want to fuck you. I've been thinking about how I was going to seduce you all day, I've thought about it all these years.'

He's only giving me crumbs of the affection I yearn for.

It confuses me but I couldn't go back there again so easily.

I know he's disappointed as he kisses me on the lips. 'I still want you,' he says as he gets out the car. 'Text me.'

Almost high from the encounter, I call James on my way back to my dad's.

'You need to decide what you want. Do you want to jump back into that fire again? Remember, every action has a consequence,' he tells me.

But I knew what I wanted: I wanted for everything to be normal again. I wanted my mother to be alive, for Kevin and me to be the way we used to be. I wanted to feel how I used to feel when we were newly married, when we were excited about our life together and I had no resentment towards him. Life was asking more from me, but I didn't think I had the energy to start again: I needed to go home, I had to try and make it work with Kevin.

* * *

For the next couple of days, I'm back at the house, immersed in the packing. The family home is now up for sale after forty-six years.

I hold my mother's favourite soft grey cardigan and cover my face with it, breathing in the lingering smell of her. After a few moments, I place it in my bag to take home.

'Dad, do you want to keep this?' I hold up a painting of a Spanish-looking house.

'Oh, we bought that when we were in Majorca,' he says, smiling. 'Lovely holiday, that was. Your mother and I went on a tour together.'

'I'm glad you have those memories.'

'I can't keep everything, though. Chuck it in the bin,' he says.

The number of things we have to sort through feels infinite.

'What about the dining room table? It's too big for your new place.'

I stand in front of the table, its lacquered top now dull. There's a small dark stain on it, right where my mother always sat. One afternoon, she had been sitting in her usual chair when she handed me a pot of hair dye.

'I'm going to teach you how to do this. They charge a fortune at the hairdresser,' she explained. 'You're good at painting so it won't be that difficult.'

I stood behind her nervously, holding a small brush. My mother tilted her blonde head back.

'Paint it as thick as you can at the front – that's where the grey is.'

I set to work as carefully as I can, but it isn't as easy as it looks.

'I can't get any more on,' my thirteen-year-old self said.

'Zara, don't paint my forehead, just my hair. It's a bugger to get off.'

Trying to wipe the gloop off with a towel, I realise I'm

smearing the dye even more onto her forehead. 'Sorry, Mum, your forehead is stained.'

'Oh, Zara!' She looks in the hand mirror and tries to clean it off herself.

The empty packet of hair dye lies next to her, the words 'Buxom Blonde' on the package.

'Mum,' I say, starting to giggle, 'the dye is called Buxom Blonde. Is it going to make your boobs bigger?'

'I doubt these breasts could get any bigger. Now stop laughing and get this dye off the table before it stains,' she tells me.

I had never been able to get it off completely, no matter how long she had made me scrub the table.

Touching the stain, I turn back to my dad. He has tears in his eyes. I realise I've never seen him cry before.

'All those lovely dinners your mother made, all the times we had family and friends over, it was all around that table,' he says, pointing to it.

'I know, Dad,' I say gently, 'I know.'

'Oh well, it's better someone else gets use out of it. It would just be a reminder for me,' he says finally.

* * *

The moving van arrives a few days later. Our house is finally empty.

Once they're gone I walk into every room, saying goodbye.

Somebody's Daughter

I go into my parents' room, my brother's room and then my own. Touching each door, I whisper my farewells. I'm glad no one is there to hear me.

For a long time I stand by the kitchen door, the way I've done since I was a little girl. I see my mother standing by the oven, cooking soup in batches, placing the contents in Tupperware and carefully writing on each one the date, the type of soup, when it should be eaten by. She was always prepared – we never ran out of food the way I do now, my kids yelling at me to go food shopping.

I remember once when I had finally plucked up the courage to ask her about sex.

'Nice girls, my dear, do not have sex before they are married. That's all you need to know,' she had said, sealing the lid on her barley soup.

'So you and Dad never had sex before you were married?' I couldn't imagine them doing it, nor did I want to.

'During our engagement we fooled around, but that's all we did. Trust me, Zara, it's best to let them wait, to make a man think you are the only one for him.' She winked at me, sticking another white label on the bowl. 'They need to think they are the only man…' She begins to hum, as she always did when she was cooking.

'But, Mum,' I began cautiously, 'does that mean my birth mother wasn't a nice girl? She had me before she was married.' My mother's hand slowed down, not responding for a moment.

'I don't know. I'm sure she was a very sad girl.'

'Mum, I sometimes wonder about her,' I whisper, trying not to sound too urgent.

'That's natural, I'm sure.' She mixes the soup faster.

Cassie calls as I'm finishing up my ritual and drags me out of my reverie.

'Oh, for fuck's sake, Zara, you do like to drag things out! I say good riddance to all those crap memories, your bloody brother and your father too. Slam that fucking front door hard when you leave! Make sure it's shut tight, so those memories stay in there forever.' She pauses. 'We've both come a long way, haven't we?'

Once I feel ready, I close the front door for the last time.

* * *

The next day I'm sitting having dinner with Cassie at our old local pub, The Orange Tree. It's a nice break from all the stress of moving. My brother hadn't helped, using his bad back as an excuse – I still found it hard to be around him anyway.

I call my dad to see how he's settling in. His voice sounds wrong somehow. Alarm bells are ringing.

'I have to go and see my dad. Something's wrong,' I tell Cassie.

'Go,' she says.

I hurry to his flat. He is slumped in his chair, barely

conscious. I try to talk to him, but his words are muddled. I'm shaking as I run upstairs to find a nurse.

'Please can you come downstairs,' I say urgently. 'There's something wrong with my father.'

One lady comes quickly, and takes his blood pressure.

'We need to call an ambulance.' She's trying not to alarm me but I can see the seriousness on her face. Soon the ambulance is here but my dad doesn't seem to know what's happening.

I call my brother. Despite everything, I know he should be here if the worst was to happen. I'm thankful when he arrives at the home quickly, not living too far away, and we follow the ambulance to the hospital.

Gary and I sit in the waiting room, both staring into space. They've moved my dad onto a bed where he's now being worked on by doctors and we can hear him moaning. Not so long ago we had been in the same waiting room, the three of us waiting for news of my mother.

My father is taken to the Intensive Care Unit. We follow him in. A tall, grey-haired doctor comes over to us.

'We need to perform a procedure right now. His heart is surrounded by fluid and we have to drain it. It's his only chance of survival. You need to understand that he might not make it. We have no choice but to operate.'

My brother and I agree to the procedure and anxiously return to the waiting room. I can't quite believe I'm here. After everything that I've been thinking about, and after meeting Simon, it's a slap round the face in terms of reality checks. I realise it's best I don't talk to my brother, though I feel so alone: we would just argue. Gary, however, talks to me about what we'll do if our dad passes away. But I can't seem to answer; I just let him talk. After what feels like an eternity, the doctor comes back.

'Your father made it through the surgery, but tonight will be touch-and-go. Please go home and rest. We'll call if there's any new information.'

I drive back to the hotel.

That night I dream about my father. He's floating in the sky and I'm standing below, my hands held high. My mother is above him, her hand stretched down towards him. None of us are touching. My father bounces between us like a rubber ball.

It takes three days for my father to come back to us. I have to change my ticket again to stay longer – I know it's a lot to place on Kevin, but there's nothing I can do.

'What can I tell you?' I say to him. 'My parents either die when I'm here, or they get critically ill. Maybe I should stop visiting.'

I have another sleepless night before I go back to the hospital to check on Dad. His bed is by the window, the sun warm against the glass. He looks so weak, but he manages a smile.

'Isn't it funny that my kidneys started failing as well as my heart, just like Mum's did?' He lets out a small laugh. 'The doctor told me what happened – I don't remember anything.'

'You're just a copycat.' I smile back.

'I didn't know there was anything wrong with my kidneys.'

'No, Dad, it's a surprise to us all,' I reply, tucking the blanket in around his feet.

'I'm glad you didn't inherit all our health issues. In some ways it's lucky you're adopted.'

At this I go completely still, my hands resting on the bed: I'm shocked. Dad has never acknowledged that I was adopted before, he'd never even said the word.

'Yes, Dad. I suppose that's something.'

I look into my father's eyes.

'Dad,' I almost whisper, 'do you think it's possible to love more than one person? A partner, I mean?'

There's a short silence. I regret immediately what I have just said.

'Oh, I'm sure that some people can, but not me. I only ever loved your mother. More than anyone else in the world.'

'But Dad,' I persist, 'you didn't exactly treat her well all the time. She often seemed to irritate you. I suppose that's marriage.'

'I did treat her well,' he said insistently. 'I gave her a lovely life, didn't I? Didn't I, Zara?'

I find myself pausing. 'Yes, Dad, you did. I know you loved her, and she loved you. Get some rest.'

13

New York, 2013

I remember the moment Kevin got the courage to confront the truth. It's the morning after I've come back from my trip to London safe in the knowledge that my Dad is out of hospital and getting the care he needs. I'm in a jet-lagged fog.

I'm in the small kitchen of our rented house. The kids are upstairs in their rooms. I had tried to hide in the kitchen when I heard Kevin come in, busying myself making toast. As soon as I saw his face, I knew he wouldn't let me run anymore.

'I've been thinking a lot while you were away. I know you've had a stressful time with your father,' he says firmly, 'but the reality is our marriage isn't working, Zara. It hasn't for years. No matter what's going on in your life it's always the same. We need to think about moving on. It's obvious you don't love me. We sleep in separate rooms, we don't have sex – you avoid intimacy at all costs. I know you've been seeing other men, I'm not stupid. You're making a fool out of me and I've had enough.'

Tears are welling up in my eyes, but he isn't finished yet.

'When I met you, I thought you would eventually get over your problems, but you haven't. It just goes on and on. I can't take it anymore. I'm sick of your family stuff, I'm tired of your adoption issues. Why don't you want to be close to me? What's wrong with you?'

I look at the face of the man I had fallen in love with all those years ago. He was still handsome, his dark hair now sprinkled with grey. Yet here I was, standing in the kitchen as my husband asked me for a divorce.

I had never been in a long-term relationship until I met Kevin. I didn't have a very good track record, flitting between boyfriends, never fully committing. But when I met him, it felt so different. He was not like any of the men I had ever been with before and he wanted me; he wanted a family, we both loved children. Maybe I felt that if I didn't take this opportunity it would never happen? I had felt when I met him in some ways cured of the old me. I thought by choosing him I was doing it differently; I thought that I had resolved so much, but it appears that I still have so much to do. All those years were me trying, imperfect though it may have been. No matter what he thought, I had loved him.

'I don't need saving anymore,' I say quietly, 'and you don't know what to do with that. You're suffocating me.'

'You think being married is suffocating?' he replies. 'You think your husband caring about you is suffocating?' Kevin runs his hand through his hair in exasperation. His face is hard and angry. 'That's what couples do – they live alongside each other, they care about each other. But to you it's an intrusion, it's someone getting in your space,' he spits sarcastically, no longer willing to hide his bitterness. 'I've tried and tried to understand you, but I don't. I can't do this anymore.'

We look at each other, both silent now. I take off my wedding ring and watch it spin around on the table, fast to begin with, then slowing down before coming to a stop. Kevin does the same, slamming his ring down on the table next to mine. Despite the tears falling heavily now, I feel like a weight has been lifted: we didn't have to pretend anymore. I'd been hoping that magical thinking would get me to fall back in love with my husband, but it didn't: it was over.

Neither of us can look at the other.

'We need a lawyer,' Kevin says quietly. 'You can have sole custody of the kids, I'll have them every other weekend. I understand that they need to be with you.'

I feel the panic rising in my chest, as it always did at the thought of someone leaving me. 'Adopted people never leave,' I had read it in a book years ago, 'because we know what it feels like to be left. So we push as hard as we can, until people leave us.'

I had felt angry at the time, the way that the author implied we were all the same. But now I could see the author had been right: I had pushed him so far away that he was left with no choice but to leave.

'I'll make it easy on you,' he sneers. 'I won't mention your behaviour.'

'It's not what you think,' I want to say out loud. 'It's about me, not you, I promise.' But how can I explain this internal battle? I remain quiet, a weight now lying on my chest. I had thought that somehow we would be different from everyone else, that in spite of everything we could figure it out. Instead we had failed – *I* had failed.

'I will never abandon you,' my husband had said, holding me tight. 'We're a family, this is what it means to be family.' I had felt so safe. How wrong I was.

We call in the children later that afternoon and I hold the girls as we cry together. Our son stands, trying to make sense of his parents.

'I'm leaving,' their father says in a flat, cold voice.

* * *

On the first night without my husband I take a bath, pouring in carefully my daughters' purple bubble bath. The liquid turns and rolls under the water, creating small bubbles. I step in and lean back against the cool surface of the bath, feeling the tension leave my body, my breath opening, stomach that was always so clenched releasing. My mind seems empty of all thought, frozen as though it has finally stilled. I stretch my legs, using my toes to adjust the hot water, until it almost burns. As I do so I feel years of built-up tension leaving my body.

'Hello, lovey.' It's Cassie calling in a silly voice. 'I got your text. You finally did it then?'

'I didn't do it, it was him,' I reply.

'Well, it's what you wanted. How many more years could you keep living this way?' she says half-jokingly. I can tell by her tone that she wants to make sure I'm okay.

'I know,' I whisper. 'But what am I going to do now? I'm middle-aged.'

'You are old, that's true,' she says. 'And the ugliest woman I've ever seen. But you're also what's known as a cougar, you're going to be fine.' At this we both giggle. 'You, my dear, are going to get on with life just as you always have.'

'Yes, yes. Just one step at a time, I know,' I agree, feeling a notch calmer.

'And one other thing…' Cassie says. 'Next time don't go for the nice personality, go for the man with the biggest dick.'

'Can't I have both?' I laugh.

'Don't be greedy!'

* * *

Somebody's Daughter

I'm in the car with my kids. The girls are reading silently, and for a moment I feel proud. I wasn't a bad parent under the circumstances.

'Mummy, I always knew you would get divorced,' my youngest, Anna, pipes up.

In a second my contentment is crushed. 'You *did*? How?'

'You just don't seem like the marrying type,' she continues. She sounds much older than her eleven years.

'The marrying type?' Katie says loudly from behind her book. 'What do you mean? She's been married for years.'

'She just isn't the type,' Anna snaps back to her sister. 'She doesn't like being bossed around. She stands up to Dad and he never liked that. She likes to do her own thing, sing in bands, and travel here and there.'

She carries on talking as if I'm not there, barely pausing for breath. I don't know whether to laugh or cry. Turning to me, she leans over to touch my arm and in the sweetest voice she says, 'It's okay, Mummy, I'm a strong independent woman too.'

As we arrive back home and step out of the car she pauses in front of me.

'I miss Grandma,' she says suddenly. 'Even though she was a little crazy, I miss her. I don't think she would have been happy about you and Daddy getting a divorce,' she adds, honestly.

In fact I'd been wondering about that myself. I knew my

mother would have been disappointed and blamed me as she often did when something went wrong in my life.

'Mum,' I had said a few years before, trying to defend myself as I told her about my troubles with Kevin. 'Why do you always think it's my fault?'

She handed me a cup of tea.

'I know how you are, Zara. You keep too much inside – you just can't do that in a relationship.'

'What do you mean?' I say, exasperated.

'Men want to feel like kings. They need to be pampered... and other things.' Her fair skin is reddening.

At this I start laughing. 'You mean sex, Mum.'

'Don't be so crude, Zara. Let's face it, I've never had any problems with your father.'

'I really don't want to hear about your sex life. You two never have problems because you're a slave disguised as a wife. That's not me. I never could do everything a man says.'

'Well, no wonder you're having problems.'

'I don't know what to do. I can't pretend to be someone else just to make his life easier.' I can hear the whining tone in my voice.

'But that's what a wife does, dear.'

'That's so depressing,' I pout.

'Not really,' she says bluntly. 'You just have to be practical. You have a roof over your head and a man with a good job, that's more important than what you want.'

Somebody's Daughter

I stare at my mother, taken aback. She has never spoken to me in this way before.

'I don't know what you mean.'

'Oh, Zara, I think you do! You've always put your own feelings first. You should be happy with what you have.'

The image of my mother fades. My daughter Anna holds me tightly.

'I'm sorry,' I say, stroking her hair.

'Sorry about what, Mama?'

'That I couldn't make the marriage work.'

'Well, it's your fault I can't sleep at night now that Dad has left.'

At least she's being honest.

'You're right,' I answer, 'it is my fault.'

Shrugging her shoulders, she hugs me tighter and then wanders off to her room.

I'm steeped in guilt and shame. Kevin was right not to trust me. It was not that I wanted to break up our family, or anyone else's, I'd been seduced again by the smiles of handsome men. But I didn't want to leave Kevin for any of them, I just liked the attention, the chase, the lust. I had tried to justify my behaviour by saying I was lonely, that the gulf in our marriage was insurmountable. The truth was that the meaningless flirting left me feeling even lonelier.

14

London, Winter 2013

I'm back in London. After spending the day with my father, I'm standing in front of Simon's door, ringing the bell. I'm late.

He opens the door, and as always, my heart flips in my chest when I see him.

'Finally you're here.' He sweeps me into his arms and carries me inside, and suddenly he's kissing me. 'I've been waiting for you. Let me look at you.'

I'm dressed simply, but with thigh-high stockings underneath.

'You drive me crazy.'

'And you drive me insane, for other reasons.'

His hands are all over me. He lifts up my skirt, turns me

around, and pushes me over the straight-backed chair in front of him so he has a good view of my bottom.

'Don't I even get a cup of tea?' I ask.

'*Tea*?' he sniggers.

'It's been a long time. Don't look too closely, things aren't quite the same as they used to be.'

'Zara, for goodness' sake shut up!' He pushes himself against me. 'You've been a very bad girl, keeping me waiting like this. You deserve a good spanking.'

'Oh, not that again! It's you that should be spanked.'

'How can you still do this to me after all these years?'

'Slow down,' I demand.

Soon we're lying down on his bed as he pushes himself inside me, kissing me with his whole mouth. Later, we fall away from each other and lie side by side. He is breathless.

'You're out of shape, old man.' I smile, looking at his face.

He smiles naughtily. 'You really are asking for it…'

'You're sick in the head,' I say.

'Oh, really?' he laughs. 'And you're the epitome of mental health. That's why you keep coming back for more.'

That's how it started. I had said to myself that I needed to visit him just one more time, but once we had made love I couldn't seem to say no. We started seeing each other in America and in London.

* * *

Months after our first meeting, I'm in bed with Simon, watching TV. It's a detective show. The husband onscreen is promising his wife that he's not having an affair. He's lying. An uncomfortable silence hangs between us. We had never used the word 'affair' – Simon thought that if he never said it, it meant we weren't having one. As the scene is playing out, he says, 'The wife always knows.'

'Oh yes, we women always know. We're smarter than men about these things, and better liars,' I reply.

'If my girlfriend ever found out, I would blame you, say you made me do it.' He is smiling now.

'I know,' I respond. 'You'd throw me out in a second to save yourself. How sad is that?'

'What's sad?' He pulls me towards him.

'That even though you would disown me in a second, I still come back.' My body is tingling again as I feel him harden next to me.

'I would miss you if you didn't.' His hand slides between my legs.

We sleep with our arms intertwined, just as we've always done. In my dreams I see myself and Kevin, driving in his car; Samuel is in the backseat. We look so young. I awake in a cold sweat, Kevin's name on my lips. I lie in the dark for a moment.

'Zara,' Simon whispers. 'Come here.'

When I lay my head on his chest, he puts his arm around

me. I breathe in his scent and feel myself relax. I had been starved of touch for so long. If this was the only place I could get it, then it would have to suffice for now.

I give myself to him, knowing that soon I will have to stop. Soon, but not right now – I'm not ready for another loss.

* * *

We spend the next day walking around Camden Market, picking up trinkets. Simon walked on the opposite side of the street from me, though, paranoid someone would see us together. We would bump into each other at market stalls as if by accident. But once in the car, he can't keep his hands off me.

'Simon, you're like a dirty old man.'

In his bedroom, I slip off my clothes and pace around the room, swaying my hips. 'So, mister, you want this ass?' I say in a mock New York accent. 'You can't afford it. I want cash. Cash only, you hear me?'

'Yes, ma'am,' he says, playing along.

'You want a picture? That'll cost you more. Jewellery is fine too.'

I walk over to him and straddle his hips.

'Cash first.' I hold out my hand.

He rolls his eyes in amusement.

'You owe me for treating me so awfully when I was young. How could you do that?'

'That was twenty years ago!' He's laughing as I pin his arms above his head.

'I don't care. You deserve to be punished.' I tease him, enjoying every minute of it. I kiss him on his full mouth. That night we're lying together in the dark.

'Simon,' I begin tentatively, 'don't you think it's weird that we still like each other?'

'Not really,' he says.

'I usually go off men so fast, and yet with you I haven't.'

'That's because you don't live with me.' His voice is gentle. 'But I don't want you to get confused. I can't give you any more than this, my girlfriend would be devastated if she knew.' He has become quiet, serious.

'So stop,' I say, a little defensively.

Holding me tighter, he whispers in my ear, 'Stop seeing you? But who else would dress up in these ridiculous outfits for me?' He pauses. 'I do think about you when we're not together. You know that, don't you?'

'No,' I whisper back, 'I don't know, because you never tell me.'

Kissing the top of my head, he says softly, 'Go to sleep, crazy girl.'

The next morning, I tell him that I'm heading for a divorce. I can hear he's angry.

'I told you to stay married and keep seeing me. I've told you, I can't give you any more than what we have now.'

His words make me feel empty, but I don't express it. Why did I think it would be different this time? I'm angry with myself for being back in this with him.

I call James. 'Your self-esteem is back in the toilet,' he tells me frankly. 'Zara, he doesn't care about you the way you want him to. He's made that clear. You just have to face the divorce head on.' He is gentle; I know he's right.

'So, no annihilating myself with drugs until it's over then?' I laugh sardonically.

'No,' he says. 'You've lost that right. Just keep your knickers on, stay away from bars, and trust that a higher power will carry you through. You've been through worse. Just take things one moment at a time.'

15

New York, March 2014

Friends had told me that they felt great relieved when they finally got divorced, but it's different for me. I'm sitting before a judge, my soon-to-be ex at a table nearby. The judge reminds me of my father, who had sat in the same position for so many years, and I feel afraid. I feel tears begin to appear from the moment I sit down, as they read out the date of our marriage, the names of our three children. All the good memories flash in my mind, the excitement of our wedding, and the joy of meeting each new baby.

I glance at Kevin. His face is expressionless, emotionless; he is good at hiding what he feels. I wish so much that I could switch off that part of me, but I can't. The judge bangs his gavel and the sound echoes through the chamber.

Somebody's Daughter

In the blink of an eye, eighteen years of marriage have come to an end.

'I thought you wanted this divorce,' my lawyer says as she hands me a tissue.

'No one wants a divorce, sometimes life doesn't give you any choice,' I say.

As Kevin and I walk to our separate cars, I wonder how long it's going to take to get used to being single again. I sit for what feels like hours, just holding onto the steering wheel, looking out into the distance at what my life has become. As I work up the courage to drive away, Cassie calls – always when I need her.

'So, how did it go? I can't believe you're really divorced. Watch out, single men of America!'

'It was awful,' I respond. This time I can't laugh at her jokes. 'I'm scared,' I add. I sound like a child.

'We're all scared. You'll be okay, it's time to stop living in half-relationships,' she tells me. She is being strong for me.

'I know, I know,' I reply.

'Maybe it's time to start doing something differently,' she says gently.

'Thank you, therapist Cassie. I will take that into consideration.'

Wrapping myself in my blankets that night, looking out at my skylight window, the moon shining in spreads a little light on my bed. I think about my mum looking down from the stars and wonder what she would have made of all of this. Falling into a restless sleep, I dream that I'm walking down the road. It's so cold, my face is freezing, my skin aching… I rummage for a moment in my deep coat pockets for a handkerchief; pulling one out, blowing my nose, I notice how soft the material is, looking carefully at the handkerchief. When I see that it's one of my father's white dirty handkerchiefs I let out a sound of surprise, wondering how it had found its way into my pocket.

* * *

The next morning, the first day of the rest of my life, it's snowing, taking us all by surprise. Despite Cassie's words, a veil of depression is lying over me. I know I have to get moving, but all I want to do is stay curled up in bed, feeling sorry for myself.

The house is still, the children asleep. I haven't told them that the divorce is final. *Do they need to know?* I ask myself. Putting on my coat and boots, I pad carefully across the snow-blanketed garden, stopping in the middle. Turning my face upwards, I let the snowflakes fall on my face. I find myself shouting to the sky.

'It wasn't supposed to be like this! We were supposed to grow old together! I've fucked it all up, Mum!' I hear myself yelling. 'Mum, where are you?'

My words are muffled by the wind.

'I don't know what to do. Mum, what do I do?'

I close my eyes.

'Then do nothing,' I hear her say back to me.

But I don't know how, I think.

'You will learn. You have to trust, my love,' she whispers. As I open my eyes, I'm sure I catch a glimpse of her face, high up amidst the snow.

I spend much of the next few days in bed, a deep depression enveloping me. Each morning, I somehow manage to get the girls ready and drop them off at school, but as soon as I'm home I either lie on the bathroom floor crying, or curl up inside my bed. I can feel bile rising in my stomach. After all, as Kevin told me, I had asked for this. I long to go back to England. I have no regular work and it's filling me with anxiety. Recently, I was let go at a school where I was working as a pre-school music teacher. I loved being with those little children. They kept me sane and in the moment during those days leading up to the divorce no matter how I felt, when I walked into school they would be so happy to see me. Their hugs and chatter lifted my spirits.

I'm so grateful for my music that I can write and put all these emotions somewhere.

'Do what's in front of you,' my friends tell me. 'One step at a time, one moment at a time.'

I feel like I'm back in early recovery, where I'm walking

blindly. I know things will change, but I wish it would all hurry up.

I open the window, feeling the cool air on my face, watching each full raindrop fall and split as it hits the ground. How mysterious is life that a person can be in the deepest pain, going through something so difficult and yet the world just keeps on turning. Shouldn't the earth stop spinning for a moment, or at least pause and acknowledge what one was feeling, a death, a break-up, a birth? But then again, I think if the earth had the manners to do that for each person, the world would stop turning altogether.

When they get home from school, the girls jump into bed with me. Their cold feet and faces brush against me. I let them see me cry.

* * *

The months are rolling on and we are all trying to adjust. Samuel is getting ready to leave high school to go to college. He is full of rage. It's so strained between us. I know he needs to leave, no matter how much I will miss him. It's time for him to leave and find himself and make sense of what has happened in his family.

I still believe that Kevin and I should stand together as a couple for the sake of the children, but it's not easy. How can it be the same? It can't be. I know I have expectations. Kevin makes it very clear he does not want to be around me, he withholds all emotion. I keep thinking we can be friends, but it's too soon.

When Samuel comes home he is still angry and decides to stay with his father. I understand, but it still hurts.

'It will change in time,' Terry tells me.

'Will it?' I'm not convinced – I'm blaming myself for everything and it's exhausting.

'You were always good at giving yourself a good thrashing.' James is trying to lighten my mood as I call him in tears. 'Zara, it is what it is. Be gentle with yourself, keep it in the day.'

'Well, I suppose it's only fair,' I tell Cassie one night when my heart feels like it would truly break. 'When Samuel was little, he only wanted me. I used to feel bad for Kevin then. Now maybe it's Kevin's turn to know what that feels like.

'But Cassie, I can't take my own son refusing to speak to me. I feel like my right arm has been cut off. I can't believe what I've done.'

'For fuck's sake, Zara!' Her frustration with me is clear. 'People get divorced all the time. Kids have to blame someone. I promise he'll come back to you.'

'Will he?' I'm not so sure – I feel like such a fool. 'I wish my mother were alive so I could talk to her,' I cry to Cassie down the phone.

'Zara, she probably wouldn't have been as helpful as you like to remember. Now go to sleep, and stop trying to solve all your problems at once. I have to go – I have a date and I've put on ten pounds. Nothing fits anymore. Call me tomorrow.'

* * *

Three weeks later, Simon comes to New York for a meeting. My mood is brightened by the thought. I end up spending the night with him. That night, I show up in a PVC nurse's outfit, my fur coat covering me to enhance the surprise. Thigh-high stockings and a tight plastic dress cling to my body; I look like a leftover rock star from 1977. The tacky look always drives Simon mad. As I take off my coat, I say, 'It's time for your medicine.' We can't stop laughing. I let him take some pictures for his collection, which turn out badly – I look like some street tramp. I sit on top of him, unpopping the dress, and start kissing him firmly until he responds. I feel him hard against me, my mouth exploring every part of him. In that moment I knew that I had him, but I knew it would only ever be for a moment. He didn't talk, which was unusual. I kept kissing him, I loved kissing him... I pushed away thoughts of my ex-husband. I'd been a coward, not wanting to be the one to face our problems. I had just run away, trying to maintain normality.

Simon pulls me back, looking into my eyes. There's a question in his eyes, but he doesn't say anything. I want to cry to curl up with his arms around me. I need him to hold me tight and tell me everything is going to be all right, but I have rarely shown my vulnerable side around him. Instead I smile to try and hide the tears I can feel surfacing and pull him into me, pushing away the feelings. As we lie together afterwards, our sweaty bodies mingled together, he strokes my hair gently. He kisses the top of my head, as he often does, like I imagine a father would to his child.

'What's wrong, Zara?' he says, not looking at me.

'The divorce is final.'

I turn to look at his reaction. He is silent for a moment. I feel an immediate distance from him.

'Well, that's what you wanted,' he says.

'Does anyone really want this?' I reply.

'I told you, Zara, you should have kept fucking him.' He stuffs a pillow behind his head. 'How could you expect a man to stay with you if you wouldn't? I told you, stay with him and keep seeing me.'

Moving away from him, I prop myself up on one elbow.

'What?' I'm in a state of disbelief. 'You think a woman should have sex with her husband even though there's nothing between them emotionally? You think she can feel close to a man who criticises her every move? You really think she should have sex regardless of all that?'

'Yes,' he says firmly.

'You are so fucking 1950s! I know you're older than me, but you actually think that?'

'Yes, Zara, I do. You gave the man no choice. It's your fault that your marriage ended.' He isn't looking at me now, instead busying himself with his phone.

I'm in shock. As I sit up in bed, naked beside him, my fury is now palpable. 'Maybe I'm just not like you, maybe I can't fuck people I have no feelings for. This is a joke! If you care about Kevin's feelings so much, why don't you call him up and tell him you chased his wife, that you fuck me as much and often as you can? That you take photos of my body and send me dirty texts?'

Standing up, I grab the nurse's outfit from the floor and squeeze myself into it. Tears stream down my face. I had never let him see me like this before.

'You don't have to start crying,' he mutters. 'You made your choice and now you have to live with it. I didn't say anything that wasn't true.'

'I really hate you sometimes,' I yell. 'You're so fucking selfish, it's always about you. You take no responsibility for your part in any of this, you never have. I hate men! You're all a bunch of wankers.'

I can see him smiling.

This isn't funny. Where's my fucking nurse's hat?'

He points to the floor, his face solemn again. Grabbing my bag, I walk away. He texts me the moment I've reached the lift.

'Zara, please come back. Don't go home.'

Pausing, my tirade of emotions stilled, I stop. I'm so tired. I make him wait a few minutes. Another text: 'You can't leave, you look completely ridiculous in that outfit.'

I walk back to his room. He's lying in bed, grinning at me. I jump on top of him, grabbing a pillow, and hit him over and over. Then we kiss slowly, and he's so tender. That night, we sleep wrapped around each other. In the morning, it's the same old routine: he leaves, as always, and I don't know when I'm going to see him again. But one thing is becoming clear: if I want to find some peace, I have to look deeper within myself.

16

New York, 2015

It's been eighteen months since Kevin left. Some level of normality is returning. The first time the girls go to stay with their dad I'm a mess. They've only been gone an hour and already I miss them. I'm not sure what to do with myself. I spend most of the evening trying to breathe and calm my forever-spinning mind. I surrender to the silence.

Many of my divorced friends have gone on Match.com. They urge me to do it straight away, but it's not for me: I'm in no hurry for a full-time relationship, I'm just not ready. I feel such a physical ache at the separation of our family. I miss our dog, who has stayed with Kevin. It's so quiet. I wonder if I wouldn't feel so lonely if I were in London. I crave home, but I have to stay for the kids – it was part of the divorce agreement and I know it's the right thing for them. The first week, I have a panic attack. I lie hyperventilating on the bathroom floor, but I don't call anyone. I still can't bear for anyone to see that side of myself.

We're living in an upstairs apartment. It's just a stepping-stone until we move somewhere nicer. I couldn't stay in the old house – the neighbours had been distant and unsupportive. When you go through a divorce, people move away from you, the invitations slow down. I'm not sure why. Maybe we divorced people are a reminder that this could happen to them. I had one neighbour whisper to me that I was the brave one. And there I was, thinking she had a perfect marriage. I know people felt the same about mine.

A few weeks ago, I started meditating daily – I didn't know what else to do with all these feelings that seemed to wrap themselves around me. I couldn't change what had happened, the mistakes I'd made. My whole life I've struggled to be gentle and kind to myself. Someone told me about Esther Abraham Hicks, a spiritualist who talks about how our thoughts determine our lives. I listen every night, and she gives me hope. I find myself worrying I'll never be able to change my thoughts, that I'll never be happy. But it's a comfort, another way of connecting with something greater than myself. Right now I haven't a clue what I should be doing. Every day I meditate and work diligently on changing these negative thoughts; I'm trying to do an inside cleanse.

Before the divorce, I had written a one-woman show. After my mother died, the dreams about my birth father took me by surprise. I didn't know he was still on my mind, but obviously he was. For many years I had avoided talking about men. I had put all my energy and focus into being a mother, and working on my relationship with my adoptive mother. Now left alone with my dad, I'm forced to have more contact than I ever had before. Until my mother died, we rarely spoke to each other. Here I am, in my forties, communicating with my father for the first time. I decide that if I'm never going to meet my birth father, I will write about what it feels like not to know. I will heal my lack of fathering using my art. Dramatic though that sounds, my play is hitting a nerve with many people and I love acting.

It's 11am and the kids are at school. I'm sitting at my computer, working on my play. For the last few days, I've noticed the power going on and off as the winds have kicked in. That's normal for our town. The houses here in Montclair are old and beautiful. We have lived here for ten years now. It might be the most artistic and diverse city in the States, but the electrics are shoddy. I'm supposed to go into the city, but I decide to stay home: the sky is turning grey and higher winds are expected. Then I notice a burning smell. I stand up, fear creeping in, and go downstairs to check the rest of the place. I don't see anything wrong, but decide to call the landlord's handyman.

'Hey, it's me. I smell burning. I think you should come over.'

'I can't,' he says. 'I'm stuck with my head in a sewer! Call the landlord.'

But my landlord isn't picking up and the smell is getting stronger. A popping noise has started coming from the walls. I stand still, unable to move.

What's going on?

The sound gets louder and louder, like fireworks. My body has gone into high alert. I turn my head and see flames jumping out of the plug socket. For a second, I can't move – I can't believe what I'm seeing. The fire rapidly grows ever higher and crackles all around me. My computer is right next to the flames.

'No!' I shout at the fire. 'Get back, I need my computer!' With shaking hands I grab it. I wonder if I should grab the kids' computers too. Should I get my guitar? My favourite pair of jeans? But my inner voice is screaming, 'Get out of the house, now!' I can't remember the number I need to dial: 999? No, that's England. What is it in America? I can't remember. Finally, I punch in 911.

'911, what's your emergency?'

'The house is going to explode.'

'Okay, Miss, calm down. Where are you located?'

I give the operator my address.

'Please vacate the property. Get everyone out, including any animals.'

Thank goodness I didn't have my dog with me.

I run downstairs and bang on my neighbour's door. He grabs his little dog and we get outside as quickly as possible. I can see smoke pouring from the window of my attic room. *Everything I own is in that room, all my lovely clothes and shoes*, I think to myself, aware of how shallow I am at times. Six fire engines show up and the firefighters run into the building. My other neighbours are saying that their houses had no power and they also smelled smoke. *Is the whole street about to go up in flames?*

Later, when everything is calm, I'm allowed back inside. Everything I own is covered in a thin layer of soot. I stand there, trying to take it all in. I don't cry; I just can't believe it. My guitars are ruined. My bed is soaked and covered in dust from where the ceiling caved in. I see the blackened remnants of my desk.

The landlord arrives: he wants to blame me for the fire. I'm in a state of shock – I don't understand how this can happen to me on top of everything else. Thank goodness for my insurance. Everything worth saving is taken away to be cleaned and the rest put in a pile to be thrown away. The marital bed I kept after the divorce has been ruined by the fire. Now all the remnants of my marriage have been wiped away, it really is time to start over.

17

London, 2015

'You're laughing,' Cassie says, as we sit together in a café in London. 'You're feeling better, I can tell.'

'Am I? Maybe I'm just getting used to my new life as a single, middle-aged woman.'

'You're free now,' she says, moving towards me in her seat. 'You can go and shag whoever you like and there's nothing to feel guilty about. I'm jealous.'

'I don't know why – you shag whoever you want and I don't think you've a guilty bone in your body,' I tell her, moving to take another bite of cake. 'There are two kinds of people, the ones who can lie without it affecting their lives and the ones who can't. You're just like him,' I add between mouthfuls.

'Oh, now that's a dig.' Cassie shakes back her dark hair,

just like she used to when she was a little girl. 'Please don't compare me to Simon, the love of your life, or the shag of your life. Let's face it, if you were with him night and day he'd drive you mad and then you'd be the one he was cheating on. When the mistress becomes the wife, there's a vacancy.'

'She's not his wife. Maybe she turns a blind eye,' I mutter. 'How could she not? But why does she stay?'

'Because they love each other, and it's easier than leaving.' Cassie looks me directly in the eye, sipping her coffee. 'Men like that are weak,' she states. 'And selfish. I know you don't want to hear it, but you need to. Everything in your so-called relationship has always been about him, on his time frame. He didn't even call you on your birthday. I'm sorry, Zara, but don't you think it's time to turn things around?'

'He told me he might be separating from her. He's unhappy, he needs me.'

'Zara, what's important is what makes *you* happy.'

I text Simon to remind him that I'm here, the way I usually do, but the reply is not what I expect.

'I'm a married man now. I can't do this anymore.'

I feel sick to the stomach. It takes me a moment to absorb what I'm reading.

'What? You didn't tell me you were getting married. I thought you were splitting up? That the relationship was over? That's what you told me.' My hands are shaking.

'I didn't know then. It all happened rather quickly.'

'What, in the last three weeks? Did she drag you down the aisle? How could you keep texting me and say nothing? Do I really mean that little to you?'

I'm furious; I feel so betrayed. We text back and forth rapidly, Cassie interjecting with what she thinks I should say.

'Let's meet,' he texts. 'We need to talk.'

But I realise the only reason he wants to meet me is because he's scared I'll say something to his new wife.

'I don't want to see you again.' I'm crying hard, I'm so embarrassed.

'Stop being so dramatic, Zara,' he texts. 'I never promised you anything.'

He's trying to control me, but I stand firm. The truth is he never cared about me. For him it's only ever been about sex. I'm reeling. I feel like I've been slapped in the face, woken from a stupid, stupid dream. Why had I allowed myself to be treated this way? Was this all I deserved? I feel betrayed, not just by him but also by myself. He keeps texting, asking to meet me, but I don't respond – I can't let him see me this way.

I can't do anything that evening. Cassie lets me sit on her bedroom floor and cry, comforting me as best she can. I cancel my plans, and as I go back to my cousin's house where I'm staying, I say nothing to them. As I lie in bed that evening in their attic room, I'm a little surprised that mingled in with my sadness is a sense of relief: it was over. Simon had done what I probably never could have.

Somebody's Daughter

I deserved much more, didn't I?

Part of me can't believe it. I call Terry and he lets me sob until I have no more tears left in me. But as I learned so many years ago when I first got sober, it's never too late to start over. Finally, I close my eyes. I'm dreaming again. This time I'm in a shop, walking up and down each aisle, looking at shoes, boxes and boxes of endless shoes. It takes me a moment to recognise that they are all my mother's shoes. I touch them gently, lifting each one. I notice the shape of her foot still imprinted in those familiar shoes, some that she had kept for many years.

I hold a soft leather shoe, one that I had played dressing up in as a child – it used to be so big on me. I lay it alongside my foot, but they were now too small. My feet had been larger than my mother's since I became a teenager. Our bodies were different in every way. Confused, I keep walking, touching the shoes. Then I stop, and I'm standing by the dressy shoes that she wore to my wedding, a light pink satin with jewels. How she loved those shoes. How she had loved choosing her dress, so excited her daughter was finally getting married, that she was finally doing something normal.

I hold the shoe against me, rubbing the satin between my fingers. What would she think now? That the wedding had been a waste of money and a waste of time.

'Excuse me, Madam,' A woman's voice is behind me. 'Can I help you with something?'

'Oh, it's okay, I'm just looking,' I say, not turning round.

'Let me know if you need anything. I'm always here, you know.'

That voice, that high lilting voice… Turning slowly, I see the back of the lady, the pink glistening mother of the bride dress, her coiffed grey hair.

* * *

Cassie comes to see me the next morning.

'The Queen has arisen,' she smirks. 'Your hair looks awful, you need to get your roots done. I didn't know you were so grey.'

'Fuck off!' I reply.

'What are you doing?' she asks.

I'm sitting on my cousin's bedroom floor, holding a box that I had taken from my Dad's. Sitting down beside me, she looks in the box and pulls out a book. She reads the title: 'The Library of Inspiration: A Collection of the World's Greatest Literature.'

'They were from my dad,' I explain. 'When I was about fourteen, he had gone out shopping and came back with books. We were standing in the kitchen when he said, "Zara, I have something for you." I was stunned. It wasn't my birthday, he'd just bought them for me because he knew I liked poetry.' I pause for a moment. 'He had never bought me a present before that wasn't for my birthday or

215

Christmas. I felt so touched that he thought of me when he was out, I've never been able to part with those books. He never ever did it again, just that one time.'

'Oh, your generous father! He should have showered his little girl with gifts.'

I smile grimly.

'Simon never bought me a present. He thought if he did, it meant we were really having an affair.'

'What did he think you were doing?'

'Who knows?' I begin to cry again, and then laugh at the absurdity of it all.

'We should sit photos of them side by side,' Cassie says. 'And place them high on your shelf. Those two tight-fisted men can keep each other company, to remind you of the little crumbs of love they signify.'

* * *

I head over to see my father in his little flat and knock loudly on the door. He doesn't hear me; the TV is at its usually deafening volume. The door is unlocked so I enter. I'm relieved that he's there.

'Oh, hello.' He smiles up at me, his frame appearing small in the large leather chair where he always sits. 'I didn't hear you. Just a minute…'

It's warm in London, almost summer.

'Dad, do you still have the heat on?' I'm sitting next to

the radiator. 'No wonder you're sweating so much. Wouldn't you feel better if you turn it down?'

'Don't touch the heat!' he yells. 'Leave it alone.'

I feel myself recoil, as I always do when he raises his voice. He has mellowed with age, but still has his moments of anger. We sit silently for a moment.

'Make us a cup of tea?' he asks, gently this time.

We spend the afternoon talking about nothing in particular, the usual surface-level conversations. His back is bent and twisted as he tries to heave himself out of the chair to go to the bathroom, a walker now needed for every move. My strange, distant father is now so vulnerable. It's hard for me to watch. Now that his body has begun to let him down, he can no longer hide his emotional fragility. It's his turn to panic, reaching out to me like a child as he approaches the end of his life.

I have a clear choice: I could punish him for his past behaviour, or be there for the person he is now. Now though, I feel compassion for this man, although he has caused me more hurt than he can ever imagine. I know he has no idea of the effects his behaviour has had on me. I always longed for the impossible. Despite everything, I still want him to act like a father.

'If you like, I could take you out to dinner one night, Dad?' I hear myself say gently.

'We'll see. I'm not sure I want to go out.'

'Have you been downstairs to join in any of the entertainment? They have a quiz night and music.'

I straighten out his papers as I talk.

'Not much – they're full of old people who never speak,' he grumbles. 'But I did meet a new friend.'

'I'm so glad you gave it a try, you might enjoy yourself.'

He makes a face like a child.

'You might need to be the one to start the conversation. You always let Mum do the talking.'

'I didn't let your mother do the talking,' he replies, finally a small smile on his face. 'She wouldn't stop talking, and no one could have made her. Maybe if she had met the Queen she would have been quiet, although I'm not sure about that.'

I laugh.

My mother's face is looking at us both from a photo on the side table. I pick it up.

'Dad, I love this picture. It really captures her personality. You can almost hear her laughing, can't you?'

'Yes.' He smiles wistfully. 'I miss talking to her, Zara. Sometimes I still chat to her while I'm watching television. I miss her so much.' He turns back towards the TV.

'Go downstairs and find some company, Dad. It will be good for you. Other people here have lost their spouses. It might make you feel better to talk about it.'

'Okay, Zara,' he says to my surprise. 'I will... Soon.'

18

New York, November 2015

We have moved into a lovely new flat. The children are happier. Both my girls are now at high school, Anna a freshman and Katie a junior. They can walk to school. We love the neighbourhood. There is a bagel shop right opposite that they keep running over to. I had been told that it takes at least two years after a divorce for things to be normal again, and it had taken two years to get this right. I didn't want to hear it at the time, but it was true. I had underestimated how long the adjustment would take. But here we are, celebrating Christmas in our new home. Life is feeling better.

A few months earlier I had been at an adoption conference – I attended them regularly now. I sat in a room listening to a man talk about a new DNA organisation, 23andMe. This is another organisation, alongside Ancestry, that has been set up as a way to connect with family members. After spitting in a test tube they can predict your ethnicity and match you up with other family members who have also taken the test. There is now a way to test both sexes with an autosomal test, so a woman can now get matched with their paternal side. It used to be just the male who could take a Y chromosome test father to son/son to father but this new test, where both male and female share the DNA, can link the woman to the male side, opening up the possibilities for women to finally find their fathers. The speaker intrigued me so much that when the time came for him to answer questions, I walked straight up to the microphone.

'Hi, I'm British, and I wondered if you'd had any luck with Europeans taking the DNA test?'

(After I had been to the Italian festival in Clerkenwell Road in London, I joined a page on Facebook for Les Enfants Terribles, the club where my birth parents had met. But I had no luck in finding my father, or anyone who knew him and I knew the whole thing was a bit like looking for a needle in a haystack. I hadn't thought about my birth father for a while after that, accepting that the likelihood of finding him after all this time would be very slim but I'd been hearing some stories and the DNA tests were inspiring me to think about searching again.)

'I'm afraid not. Europeans don't tend to do them. Our database shows us it's mainly Americans,' the speaker told me.

At this my heart sank. However, it seemed new discoveries in DNA were changing things for the adoption community. The speaker advised me to sign up and take a test on Ancestry.com, as they have a bigger database. So I did, later that same day, and sent off a sample of my spit. I was put in touch with a woman called Gaye – who I now call my 'DNA search angel' – whose job is to then pool my results together from the three main sites that now exist: Ancestry, 23andMe and Family Tree DNA. I told myself I wouldn't get my hopes up, after all my previous searches, but when my results came back, I couldn't help but be excited – they show that I really am Italian. After all this time, I just knew it. It made it all the more real, like beginning again.

19

London and New Jersey, 2016

It's been two years since my journey has started. The girls are with Kevin and I'm back in London on my own, performing my one-woman show, *Beneath My Father's Sky*. I've now been performing the show for three years. I've been all over the States with it and I've been so happy with the response.

So many people are coming tonight, old friends I haven't seen in years. Once again I'm staying with my cousins from my adoptive mother's side. We have become closer since our mothers died. It helps me stay connected to that side of our family. I don't invite my adoptive father, nor do I tell him I'm performing the show – at his age, I don't think he should have to deal with this. We have never discussed that I have a biological father out there somewhere. I know he sees me as his daughter, and he is the only father I've ever known.

A Soho-based website publishes an article on my search for Antonio, my birth father. Someone who knew him might read it and contact me, I think, although at the moment, I'm more focused on my show than finding him.

I'm nervous as I wait backstage. All my friends and some adoptive family are coming. I wish my cousin hadn't invited them. I know she means well, but she has already told me off for having photographs of my parents as part of the set. She feels the play is too revealing, that I'm not letting my father defend himself. But I'm not sure what he needs defending from. I'm irritated that she would bring this up when I'm about to go onstage.

'You knew what this play was about, you read the script ages ago. I don't understand why you would say this to me now.'

'I just didn't realise how intimate it would be. I'm not comfortable with this, I think you should take down his photograph.'

'No, it's part of the play. And many people here know what he looks like. I need to get ready to go on.'

She needs to go. I want to push her away from me, but I have to focus.

I can hear that the room is full. I know my birth mother and sister are here too. As I sit backstage, my nerves are increasing more and more. Anger rises in my stomach, as it always does when I'm made to justify myself to someone. I need to give this all I've got. It's time to tell my story, I walk out onto the dark stage…

* * *

They seem to have enjoyed the play. I spot an ex-boyfriend from when I was fifteen seated way in the back. My friends beam at me. I see the line of adoptive cousins a few rows back.

It's time for the question and answer panel. My cousin comes to facilitate. One of my aunts asks the first question.

'Are you ever going to get over this? Will there ever be closure?' Her voice is pompous. I pause for a moment, considering how to answer.

'No,' I tell her directly, 'I won't ever get over losing my biological family and not knowing who my father is, but I still live a productive life.'

'*Are* you?' she says loudly.

I'm furious. The crowd is silent.

'I'm an artist.' *Why do I even try and explain this*, I think to myself. 'This is the work I do. I write about it, perform it to others, and try to educate people.'

I'm rescued by an adoptee, crying in the audience, who says that the play touched her. Thank goodness, this is a tough crowd.

Somebody's Daughter

I look over at another aunt, who I can see wants to tell me the same thing: that I'm overreacting.

'This is my story, why are you trying to make it yours?' I say quietly and calmly.

At the end of the show the room is full of old friends coming to say hello. I feel depleted but content – I know I did the best I could. As I arrive back at my cousin's house later that evening, I'm greeted by all of them seated silently around the kitchen table.

'Vicky is furious. She feels you ignored her completely. None of them are happy,' my cousin says, without so much as a hello.

'Ignored? I had eighty people to say hello to! I invited them to the green room and they didn't come. I'm tired of this.' I want to cry – I feel unsupported, the way I always did around my adoptive family.

'Well, we all feel that the reason you feel the way you do,' my cousin continues, 'is because you had a very difficult time with your dad and brother. If you had been raised differently, you wouldn't feel this way.'

'You all feel that?' I'm almost laughing at the nerve of them, imagining their discussion and analysis of my personality. 'I've been around hundreds of adopted people who all feel the same way I do, I'm not alone. Why is it so hard for you to understand?'

They don't get it and they don't want to. I feel like my

work has failed to explain what it's like for adopted people. I'm sinking as I stand in front of them.

'By the way, when are you leaving? Not that I'm throwing you out or anything.' My cousin has become cold.

I can't sleep that night. They have always shown kindness to me – I can't understand why it's been withdrawn so quickly. The next morning, I get up early and pack my bags. I go to stay with a friend. My friend comforts me as I cry. A day later, I drive to the airport. None of my adoptive cousins have tried to contact me since I walked out.

* * *

I'm back in New Jersey. It's February and the ground is covered in snow. I've sunk into a deep depression. I miss my friends back home and feel little connection to anyone here. My adoptive cousins have cast me off and I can't shake the feeling of abandonment. Once again, I feel like I don't fit in anywhere. Will I ever be fully a part of anything? I know it's all so self-pitying, but the thought has taken a hold of me.

I had given my cousin a suitcase of family photographs, which contained pictures of both our mothers. One afternoon, we sat going through them, and I told her to take the ones that she liked.

'Look at the resemblance,' she had said, gazing at yellowed photos of grandparents and aunts. 'Look, you can see my children in every face.' It was true; the family resemblance was uncanny.

'I should keep all these photographs. Let's face it, your children don't look like any of these people – how could they?'

'How can you say that? They're my family too.'

I would never truly be a full part of that family; I wasn't sure why I still cared.

* * *

Winter turns to spring, and my mood is lifting. These days I spend a lot of time writing. I've been asked to write a book based on my play for a new agent that I had been introduced to who had seen my play, but I write more than that: I write about a woman going through a divorce, I write the story of the reunion that she has with her birth father. I'm enjoying imagining what that would feel like.

'This is my way of healing,' I tell my adoption group. 'The chances of me ever finding my birth father are so slim, it seems the best thing to do is to try and make peace with it all.'

I'm tired of being sad. Another layer is being peeled back; life is asking more from me again.

'How many more layers? We must be close to the core,' I laugh with James on the phone.

'Zara, it's a lifetime of work. Now get off the cross, we need the wood! Start having some fun,' he tells me.

20

Father's Day, 2016

I haven't dated anyone since my divorce, but I went on Tinder recently after some of my friends urged me to do it. I find it so strange, flipping through photographs of men. My friends have told me I'm too fussy. But it's not a fun experience – the last guy I chatted with was young and still newly married. I was so upset that after only two years of marriage, he already wanted to cheat. I started sending him ridiculous messages.

'I think you're nice and everything, but I don't think that's your body in the photo.' The man in the picture was tanned and well-muscled, his face out of the frame.

'How did you know?' he messages back.

'Just a feeling. Why don't you want to show your face?'

'I'm married. I don't want anyone to know I'm on here.'

'How long have you been married?'

'Two years.'

'Two years and you're already having affairs?'

'Is that bad?'

'Yes, it's bad. Go fix your marriage.'

'Really? So you don't want to meet me now?'

'I'm not meeting anyone without a head! You should get off Tinder, you're young, and believe me, divorce is hard.'

I call Cassie afterwards. 'You're never going to have hot sex if you keep counselling everyone on Tinder,' she laughs.

* * *

I've decided to succumb to the bass player who's been chasing me for a while. We met a few years ago when I was playing with a group of musicians in New Jersey. He's handsome and not committed to anyone else – perfect for me right now. It's Saturday afternoon and the girls are with Kevin. The bass player is coming over. He has his clothes off in moments, and mine not long after. I'm impressed. We lie on my bed and start kissing, but my phone keeps beeping.

'Hold on.' I lean over to grab the phone. It's a text from my youngest daughter, asking if I want a piece of furniture their dad doesn't need anymore.

'Yes, I can take it.'

I lean forward and start kissing the bass player again. I'm

not sure how much time has passed when I can hear the front door open and my daughter's voice, followed by the sound of clunking and banging as if someone were moving furniture. The bass player's shoes are in my room, thank goodness. No one will know he's here.

I throw on my dressing gown, close the bedroom door and lean over the banister.

'Are you kidding me? I'm trying to nap,' I say.

Kevin is sullen at my response: 'You said you wanted the sofa.'

'I didn't say now! No one told me you were coming over this minute.'

He dumps the sofa in the basement and they both leave, slamming the front door, reminding me what a bitch from hell I am, how ungrateful I am.

I open the bedroom door, but the bass player is no longer in my bed. I search the room – how did he get out? Who is he, Houdini? I open my wardrobe door and there he is, stark naked, standing amongst my dresses with a worried look on his face. I can't stop laughing.

'I'm divorced. I'm allowed to have a man over.'

But he never comes back to my house again.

* * *

It's the night before Father's Day. I'm passing time on Facebook, scrolling through messages from the adoption group I'm a member of. I notice a few stories of adopted people finding their fathers via DNA; adopted people like me were being reunited, despite barely having any information. I smile as I read their posts – I feel so happy when I see that people are reuniting this way. *How incredible it is that DNA is so advanced that we can now find family this way*, I think to myself. I hadn't checked my Ancestry page for a long time; I'd had some matches with distant cousins, but nothing on my father's side and by now, I wasn't expecting to find anything. But something about the Facebook posts makes me curious to check again. I log into my page and immediately see a new match and a message.

Hi, looks like we're related.

I click on the icon. The match alert reads:

Predicted relationship: Close Family
Possible range: Close family – 1st cousins
Ethnicity: Italian, British, Greek

I'm stunned. I don't know what this means, but I know it means something. I message Gaye, my DNA search angel, the lady that I had met the previous year at an adoption conference, who helps adopted people decipher these new tests.

Zara Phillips

Did you see there is a possible first cousin match?
They messaged me. I wrote back to ask who they
could be. It seems that it's a very close match.

6/18, 11:23pm

Gaye Sherman Tannenbaum

Is this the match Ma258?

I thought you told me that was your half-sister in
England? Your sister from your birth mother? She is
half-Italian too so it could be her. I had seen it, but
didn't think anything of it.

Zara Phillips

I don't remember ever saying that my sister had done the
test. I am sure that she didn't do a test, but I can check.

6/18, 11:26pm

Gaye Sherman Tannenbaum

It says Close Family to First Cousin. The amount
of DNA shared is twice what first cousins share. It
usually means half-sibling, but could also be an aunt
or a grandmother.

6/18, 11:48pm

Gaye Sherman Tannenbaum

This is nothing short of amazing. From what I can see
this is a half-sibling. Let's see what your sister in England
says then we know whose side it is coming from.

6/18, 11:48pm

Zara Phillips

The message on the site is from a few weeks ago, I can't really believe it.

6/18, 11:48pm

Gaye Sherman Tannenbaum

She also logged in last week.

6/18, 11:48pm

Zara Phillips

Yes, I saw that. Shit, I haven't been on this site for ages. I just messaged my sister in London to ask if she did a test. I hope she didn't, I am sure she didn't but I have to wait and see *ugg*.

6/18, 11:50pm

Gaye Sherman Tannenbaum

Right. Unless she sent it as a joke. 'Looks like we are related...'

Gaye Sherman Tannenbaum

You also share a match with this other person. His initials are DD. He is listed as a 4th cousin match to you and your mystery match.

I wish your sister would message you back.

6/19, 12:07am

Zara Phillips

Oh, my goodness!!!!

6/19, 12:08am

Zara Phillips

I wish she would message me back too but she will be sleeping

6/19, 12:15am

Gaye Sherman Tannenbaum

Okay – I'll be up early, checking for messages. Good night!

6/19, 12:23am

Zara Phillips

Night and thanks again.

I message the mystery match again, just in case she hasn't seen the first one from me:

Hi, I'm not sure if you're seeing my messages. I was adopted and found my birth mother many years ago. My father was Italian and I've never met him. I don't know very much about him, except where he met my birth mother and where he worked, when he lived in London in the sixties. It seems that you and I are very close family. I'm not sure exactly how, but I would love to find out more about you. I see that your DNA says you're Italian too? I'm hoping we can talk more. I'm excited at the thought of knowing who you are. Please message or email me.

Zara

Somebody's Daughter

It's getting late. I'm in bed, but I can't sleep – I'm checking my phone endlessly to see if my sister in London has messaged me back, but she wouldn't have yet as it's still too early there. I'm sure she didn't do an ancestor test but I doubt myself. Overwhelmed, I get out of bed and stand in the dark in the middle of my room. The moon is shedding a tiny sliver of light. I'm fifty-one years of age. Up to this point I've spent my life with no answers as to who my birth father could be. It's been years since I met Pat, my birth mother, trying to imagine who he could be, piecing together fragments and pictures from the stories she has told me. It has seemed like an impossible search and yet here I am.

I feel an energy surrounding me in my small room as if there are many people standing together with me and I'm not alone. I know in my heart that this person is connected to my birth father – I feel it, I just know. *It's funny*, I think to myself, *how when something so profound as this happens it's like time has stood still. Only in these moments are we fully aware*. I stand in a state of disbelief as my world changes within hours. Then I hear a clear, strong voice, so loud it speaks to me as if someone were standing there in front of me.

'It's all part of the greater plan, the reason you had to wait so long.'

I can feel the tears silently rolling down my cheeks. The house is still, the children sleeping. I feel warmth and love, and a trusting feeling, the same one I experienced when I got down on my knees and asked for help with getting sober all those years ago. I'm infused with clarity.

'Zara,' I hear myself saying out loud, 'you can trust it's safe. It always has been safe, it really always has been.' Elated, overwhelmed, I'm overcome by this realisation and feel gentleness towards myself – gentle in a way that would have helped me many years before.

'You just didn't know, but here is the proof!' I'm talking out loud, whispering into my shadowy room. 'And if you don't start trusting now, you never will.' My thoughts are clear; I feel a moment of such excitement and sadness mingled into one as I think back. If I had known what today would bring, I might have felt so differently in my life. And in that moment, I knew that I was loved, that no matter how my beginnings were, how much shame I had carried because of starting my life as a bastard, a mistake, a quick fling, in spite of all of that I was loved.

Zara Phillips
Have barely slept, but no, my sister from Pat says she didn't do any test at all. Going to try and sleep some more now.
6/19, 6:34am

Somebody's Daughter

Zara Phillips

So, now that we know this is not my sister from my birth mother it must be a relative from his side?
6/19, 11:40am

Gaye Sherman Tannenbaum

This is what is known as a '25% share'. There is a short list of possibilities (in order of likelihood):
1. Half-sibling (maternal or paternal) 2. Full aunt/uncle/niece/nephew (full meaning that it was from a full sibling – your half-sister's child would only be a half-niece) 3. Grandparent/Grandchild 4. Double first cousin (you share maternal AND paternal grandparents – your mother's sister married your father's brother).
6/19, 12:19pm

Gaye Sherman Tannenbaum

That's all we know until this MA person gets back to you.
6/19, 12:21pm

Zara Phillips

Should I contact the other Italian 4th cousin DD that we both matched with?
6/19, 12:25pm

Gaye Sherman Tannenbaum

Wait a couple of days until you hear back from MA.
6/19, 12:26pm

Zara Phillips

OK, will do.

6/19, 12:27pm

Gaye Sherman Tannenbaum

Oh, and Happy Father's Day. ☺

He's definitely Italian.

6/19, 12:28pm

Zara Phillips

Thanks, ha ha, and so is she! Do we know if it's a girl?

6/19, 12:29pm

Gaye Sherman Tannenbaum

She's also Jewish and British.

6/19, 12:30pm

Zara Phillips

I know, wtf? How do you know they are a 'she'?

6/19, 12:31pm

Gaye Sherman Tannenbaum

MA has a pink icon – so female. DD has a blue icon
– so male.

6/19, 12:32pm

Gaye Sherman Tannenbaum

I've got some info on DD. He's based in the US.
He lives in New Jersey.

6/19, 12:44pm

Zara Phillips

Omg r u kidding?

6/19, 12:51pm

Gaye Sherman Tannenbaum

Remember – he's a FOURTH cousin. You can
contact him once you get the scoop from MA.

6/19, 12:52pm

Zara Phillips

I am hoping the girl tells me her father's name is …
Antonio or her uncle!

6/19, 12:54pm

Gaye Sherman Tannenbaum

We just have to wait for MA to respond.

6/19, 12:57pm

Zara Phillips

OK, but do you know what I am saying about my
birth mother, could she be connected to her? Not
sure there could be a connection as she is not Italian
at all.

6/19, 3:06pm

Gaye Sherman Tannenbaum

I'm about 80% sure it's a paternal sibling to you.
Maybe 85% sure. I know it's hard but you need to
wait for MA to respond.

6/19, 3:07pm

Zara Phillips

It is hard to wait!!

6/19, 3:08pm

Gaye Sherman Tannenbaum

Just because MA has some Jewish doesn't mean she's connected to your birth mother. It also doesn't mean that she ISN'T connected to your birth mother. If I matched with someone who was half-Jewish and half-British Isles, I wouldn't know if it was from my mother's or father's side.

6/19, 3:09pm

Zara Phillips

I know what you're saying but that would be very odd if she was and could only be really if it were another of her children. I daren't ask her if she had anymore, not sure whether to say anything to my birth mother yet or not. She could have had sex with another Italian!!!

6/19, 3:11pm

Gaye Sherman Tannenbaum

Don't say anything until we figure out who MA is. It will be very easy to see if she's a maternal or paternal sibling or something else (highly improbable that she's not a sibling, but I have to list ALL possibilities). Like I said – either your father likes Jewish women or your mother likes Italian men.

6/19, 3:17pm

Gaye Sherman Tannenbaum

If you didn't know either of your parents, the chances would be 50/50 maternal or paternal. Since you know your mother, and believe it's unlikely she had another child that you don't know about, KA is probably on your father's side. But – not impossible this is a maternal sibling.

6/19, 3:18pm

Zara Phillips

Well, I could ask her directly?

6/19, 3:19pm

Gaye Sherman Tannenbaum

MA?

6/19, 3:20pm

Zara Phillips

No, my birth mother. I could ask if she had another kid, make a joke out of it.

6/19, 3:21pm

Gaye Sherman Tannenbaum

Why make waves when you don't have to?

6/19, 3:22pm

Zara Phillips

OK, I did tell my sister I might have a relative match but will tell her not to say anything yet.

6/19, 3:23pm

Gaye Sherman Tannenbaum

Tell your sister that you think it's on your father's side and you're excited. That's all she needs to know right now. That's all you CAN tell her because you don't know either –until you get a response from MA.

6/19, 3:29pm

Zara Phillips

My sister messaged said she thinks my birth mother would be happy if we found him.

6/19, 3:31pm

Gaye Sherman Tannenbaum

That's good.

6/19, 3:32pm

Zara Phillips

Yes, I actually think she wants to meet him.

6/19, 3:33pm

Gaye Sherman Tannenbaum

One step at a time.

6/19, 3:33pm

Zara Phillips

I know he may not be alive or even want to meet me. I have thought about it all in the last 24 hours, but at least she would be OK if I searched.

6/19, 4:45pm

Gaye warns me not to get my hopes up – this potential half-sister might not know who her father is either – but my body is shaking. I have to keep telling myself that even if I find my father, he might not want to meet me. He might not even be alive.

Somebody's Daughter

It's a few trying days before Gaye gets back in touch to say that my mystery match has logged in to Ancestry so I send another message with my email, hoping for an answer.

Finally, I get an email from her:

Hi Zara,
Yes, let's talk! I live on the west coast Are you free this evening?

Best,
Michelle

I had given her my number and she didn't wait long to call me once she sent the email. That evening I was sitting in my AA meeting when I looked down to see that I have a missed call and a voicemail. I leave the room immediately and go out to the street towards my car. When I press the voicemail I hear a bright, bubbly American voice on the phone.

'Hi Zara! My name is Michelle. I just looked on my Ancestry page and it seems that you're my closest match. I'm adopted too. Please call me back. I'm free for another hour this evening.'

I call straight back, my heart racing, and it feels like talking to a friend. She immediately tells me her story:

'I was adopted, but I found my birth mother a few years ago. I just met my birth father.'

She is chatting with me so openly. My heart feels like it's going to explode in my chest. I ask her slowly, 'What is your father's name?' But I know the answer before she tells me.

'Antonio.'

'Oh my God!' I know I'm yelling into the phone but I can't seem to help it. All my inhibitions have gone. 'My father's name is Antonio. We're sisters!'

I listen as she tells me the whole story. Michelle is so kind. As an adoptee she understands how I feel – I don't have to explain anything.

'He has two sons by different women, both kept by their mothers. They live in London now. He was married to the younger one for a while. It seems the older one is close to our age.

I hurriedly begin to take notes, just in case this is the only conversation we ever have.

'Can you tell me his last name, please?' I've waited years for this information.

She spells it out clearly. I write it down a few times on my pad, not wanting to forget it, and then enter it in my phone. I don't want to lose it, although I know there's no way I could forget what I've just heard. Finally, I know my father's name. I can't quite take it all in.

'Ready for the next part?' she says.

'There's another part?' I laugh, feeling overwhelmed.

Somebody's Daughter

'He married a woman from New Jersey. They lived in California for a while, but a few years ago they decided to move back.'

'Are you kidding me? Where?' I google his town and see we only live fifty minutes' drive from each other. I'm stunned. I've performed many gigs in that area – we could have walked past each other on the street and never known we were father and daughter.

'Go on Facebook on your phone, and I'll show you how to find a photograph of him.' I can tell even she is excited.

My hands are shaking as I scroll down until I'm looking at a photo of a handsome man in a pink shirt. He has a deep tan, kind eyes and a smile that's somehow familiar. I stare at him, the same way I stared when I first saw the photo of my mother. I look at every detail. Finally, a photo of my father! I've waited so long for this.

'One of our brothers is an artist. He's very established in the art world in England. I'll send you a video. You can see photographs of Antonio when he was younger, too.'

'Thank you! Thank you for being willing to share with me.'

'You're welcome, sister! So, how do you want to proceed? I can help however you like, but only if you want me to.'

'Would you mind being the one to tell him about me? I think it would be best coming from you.'

'I would be happy to. I'll call him soon, and let you know what he says.'

I feel like I'm floating. My mind is struggling to take in all this information. In one moment, everything has changed: I'm no longer the woman who doesn't know who her father is, I know he's alive. I know what he looks like. In one moment, I have his name and I know where he lives.

I've spent fifty-one years fantasising about this man. I had spent so long trying to paint a picture of him in my mind with only the fragments available to me. There was another little girl just like me, wondering who her father was. I had a sister I'd never known – I'd never even dreamed that part of the story. In one moment, I had gained five new siblings.

As I drive home, I try and take it all in. I don't tell the children anything – I still need to come to terms with everything myself. But I sit at the computer that night, scrolling through Facebook, trying to find more photographs of Antonio. His wife is so beautiful, they have grandchildren; they are regular people, just like my birth mother. I spend a few days with my phone switched off, letting the information sink in. It takes my body time to absorb this new reality.

21

Home, July 1st 2016

Michelle calls me a few days later. She says she's told Antonio about me, but he's apparently in total shock and needs some time to take it all in. He has no memory of my mother, but agrees that the time and dates that he was in London match up. He has told Michelle that he will call me when he's ready.

Now it's time for me to tell my family, including Kevin. I tell them all that's happened and I'm thrilled at how excited they are for me. Only my son Samuel is cautious. 'Can this really be true?' he asks. I try to reassure him, but I hear the doubt in his voice. I'm grateful for his concern and understand how insane this whole story sounds. When I tell my close friends, they are so happy for me. Now all I can do is wait: it's his move.

I'm trying to be patient, and push all the negative thoughts away. I'm beginning to realise that Antonio didn't know Pat had fallen pregnant, or has simply forgotten – it's not what I'd expected, I just assumed he knew. I'm finding that truth difficult.

The days have turned into a week. He tells Michelle he just needs more time, that it's a lot to take in. I understand, but I need to hear from him desperately.

Another week goes by. *Am I not important to him at all? Is he going to pretend I don't exist? What if he never contacts me? How will I make peace with that?*

1st July: It's my youngest daughter Anna's fourteenth birthday so I take the girls out for brunch in the local café. It's a good distraction and I'm trying hard to make it a nice day for Anna despite everything that's going on.

Suddenly, as we sit down at the table, Michelle texts me.

'Antonio is going to call you now. Are you ready?'

'Now?' I respond.

'I'm at the airport, about to go away for the summer. Before I left, I urged him to call you. He will any moment, I promise.'

I can't focus.

'Girls, I know this is a special day,' I say to them both, 'but my birth father is about to call me.' I feel dizzy, my appetite suddenly gone.

'What, now? On my birthday?' Anna seems a bit put out.

'I know, I *know*. After all these years, he's going to call on your birthday.'

She smiles. 'It's fine. As long as you still take me shopping.'

The girls are reassuring. They can see I'm all over the place. Then my phone rings and a rush of adrenaline courses through my body.

'It's him!' I freeze up – I can't seem to pick up the phone.

'Answer it, Mum!' my daughters are shouting. 'Go outside, go, GO!'

I run outside. I can see the girls laughing together as they watch me through the window.

'Hello,' a deep Italian voice says to me on the phone.

'Hi.' My voice is faint. I pause.

He laughs lightly.

'I'm sure this is a surprise,' I find myself saying.

'You think? This was the biggest shock of my life! I'm sorry I don't remember your mother. Maybe if you tell me more, I will.'

I tell him the story that I've told so many people, over and over. He confirms that he used to go to Les Enfants Terribles and that he lived above a shop in Victoria, by the station. What's bothering him is that he can't remember my birth mother's name. He has no memory of a woman telling him she was pregnant.

All those years of wondering about him and he didn't

even know I existed. This is not what I expected – I don't know how to feel.

'I think we should meet,' he offers. 'You can show me a photograph of your mother and we can do a paternity test.' I agree that we should meet and he ends the call by telling me he'll call me. I walk back inside and see the looks of love and concern in my girls' eyes as I wonder if I will hear from him, or if this is the end.

* * *

Three days later, he calls.

'Come and meet me at Dunkin' Donuts in an hour, okay? Ciao, bella.'

Every hair on my body is standing on end as I scramble to get ready. I've already met one birth parent – I should be a professional at this by now. Instead, I'm panicking. What do I wear? I don't have time to think about clothes. I wish I'd planned an outfit in advance, but part of me believed the meeting would never really happen.

I call my friend Tom from the adoptees group as I start my car.

'Make sure you take photos,' he says. 'Ask him as many questions as you can, just in case this is the only time you get to meet him. Zara, it's going to be OK.'

His words are wise, calming.

'I'm going to meet my father, I'm going to meet my

father!' I yell it out loud, just to hear myself say it. As I drive along the highway, trying to focus on the road, counting down the exits, I can't focus on anything but him.

At last I turn into the parking lot. There's a man pacing back and forth, looking into each car that pulls in. I know it's him.

I step out of my car and our eyes meet as we walk towards each other. He has tears in his eyes, I can see that. He is exactly how Pat described him, except older. His eyes look so familiar, I can't stop looking into them: our eyes are the same colour. We recognise something in one another. As we walk in together I can't help but think of Michelle's text from earlier:

'Dunkin' Donuts? That's where I met him for the first time! Have one with sprinkles for me.'

We stand in the line together, trying to look like just two normal people grabbing coffee together. Every few seconds I catch him staring at my face. We sit down. I feel surprisingly at ease with him.

'Life is full of surprises…' He raises his hands to the sky and half-laughing, he says, 'How did you find me again? My wife, she's going to kill me! Divorce me!'

I show him a photo of Pat around the time they would have met. He doesn't recognise her.

'Please don't tell her,' he says quickly. 'I had many girlfriends when I was young. I'm sorry, but it's true.'

I can see he's ashamed by this admission but I don't feel any judgement towards him. I feel badly for Pat as I know this will be hard for her, though. It's easy to imagine how he was, a young, handsome Italian in sixties London – I'm sure all the girls went crazy for him.

'Antonio, we all have a past. Believe me, I was no saint.' He looks sheepish. 'Really? You too?' He relaxes a little.

'Yes, really! The only difference is, I didn't get pregnant.' He is studying me again, back in denial. 'Well, I don't know how we are related but I know that we must be somehow.'

I explain the DNA test, but I know he isn't convinced.

'Let's go and get a paternity test now. Then we'll know for sure.'

We walk into the busy street. Antonio takes my hand and pulls me across the middle of the road, in between cars. *I'm holding my father's hand.* I feel giggly. I think I held my adoptive father's hand once when I was a little girl but it's a completely different feeling now, one I never thought I'd ever get the chance of having.

We find the nearest pharmacy and walk up and down the aisles, trying to figure out where they would keep a paternity test. Antonio is looking uncomfortable, shifty. Eventually I ask a girl for help and she walks us to another section, but in front of us are pregnancy tests. I crack up laughing.

'Not pregnancy.' Antonio's voice is loud, his thick accent filling the space. 'Paternity, paternity...' He says it slowly so she understands, but between both of our accents, she's having a hard time.

'I'm sorry, we don't have any of those,' she says as she looks us both up and down.

I leave him soon after that, telling him I will arrange to meet him again once I have a test – I need to know as soon as possible. He doesn't want to say anything to his family yet. I drive off, knowing he still doubts my identity.

But I have no doubts: I know I have finally met my father.

1 Week Later

22

A Week Later

'Towels, check… Sunscreen, check… Water, check…'
My youngest daughter Anna and I are heading to the beach.

'Paternity test, check…' I throw the box on top of the bag.

'This family is beyond weird.' My daughter rolls her eyes.

I have arranged to meet Antonio back at the Dunkin' Donuts car park to get a sample of his saliva – I'm just glad he is open to this. My daughter waits in the car as I step out and he says hello to her, his granddaughter. I watch her face: she is serious and unusually quiet, observing the scene.

'I've done this before, with Michelle. I know how to do it,' he says as he opens the test and swabs the inside of his cheek before sealing it up.

'Let me know what it says, okay?' He is smiling as he leaves. My daughter has been quietly watching the whole time.

'It's definitely him,' she says. 'You're just like him.'

I've been calling Pat to keep her updated and I send her a photo of Antonio.

'It's him,' she replies. 'I told you he was handsome. He doesn't remember me, does he?' I know she's upset, I don't know what to say.

'He's having a hard time remembering that you told him you were pregnant. I'm sure it will come back to him soon,' I say, hoping to reassure her.

'Well, I told him. I know what I said, and I know what his response was – it wasn't nice.'

I feel stuck between the excitement of meeting my father and trying to support Pat. I can see her pain resurfacing – I can't blame her for being angry.

A few days later the paternity test company calls me. I'm told that the test won't work with just Antonio's sample, they need my mother to complete a test to determine if he's my father. Sometimes this happens; it depends on what DNA the child carries from each parent. I call Pat and tell her I'm sending her the kit, and ask her to courier it back to the company in the States. She agrees, but I sense she's still struggling.

Every day I check to see if the company has received

her package. Then I find out she didn't use a courier, but sent it through the Post Office. I've lost all patience. *Why is the universe testing me like this?* I can't help but feel angry towards her – it's like she's trying to stall things on purpose.

'I asked you to courier it, I don't know why you couldn't do that for me. This will take weeks, I can't wait weeks.'

'We know it's him. I don't understand why you can't wait. The courier place was too far away, I did what I thought was best.'

'We know it's him, but he isn't convinced. I need this, I can't wait anymore.'

'You've waited years. What's a few more days?'

I knew in some ways she was right, but I needed him to acknowledge me. I can't seem to focus on anything so I check the tracking number again. The paternity test is stuck in Customs. I phone Chicago and they tell me the package could be there for weeks.

I call the paternity test company and they suggest that this time they send the package to Pat direct in England. I have to pay another $200, but I don't care.

'Another kit is on its way. All you have to do is take the test. The postage is paid, and there's a DHL box near your house,' I text before giving her directions.

I send her a second text: 'Pat, I want you to know that I understand this is bringing up a lot of stuff for you. Thank you for doing this.'

Somebody's Daughter

I know she's still angry that Antonio doesn't remember her. She was seventeen years old, a child herself. She was the one who had to carry me; she was the one who was made to give me up. How any mother is able to function after such a trauma is hard to imagine. I think you would have to switch off a part of yourself just to survive.

* * *

It's now been three weeks since the beginning of the paternity test ordeal but Pat finally tells me she's sent her sample back. Antonio has even called a couple of times. He still sounds unconvinced. My friends are texting me, asking if I've heard anything – they're as anxious as I am.

I turn my phone off for a while – I need a break from my thoughts. I keep wondering if the Ancestry website has made a mistake. I did, however, buy another DNA test. I drove back to meet Antonio at Dunkin' Donuts. This time we go inside, as he has to spit in the vial. I repeat the information that my birth mother has told me. I show him a photo of me as a little girl. He studies it for a long time; he has gone silent.

'Why don't I remember? Don't you think I would remember if a woman told me she was pregnant with my child?'

I shrug my shoulders.

'I don't know what to think anymore,' I say to him.

As I leave, he says, 'Well, maybe we're related, maybe we

aren't. I'm glad to have met you either way. Let me know as soon as you know, okay?'

'Antonio,' I smile. 'You will be the first one I call.'

I drive home in the intense summer heat. What if the paternity test fails? What if there's a problem, and he never believes that I'm his daughter?

* * *

The girls are staying with their father that night so I'm alone and glad of it – I'm finding it hard to be focused and present as a mother right now. I've hidden how I feel from the children, from a lot of people, but how can I explain what it feels like to sit with this man I know is my father, and for him to still be unsure? I'm still battling with the fact he didn't remember Pat, my whole conception.

Friends tell me, 'But you know it's him.'

But I need him to know in his heart that I'm his daughter.

I lie on my bed; it's late. I'm starting to have that old familiar feeling, the one I had as a little girl when some nights I would feel sadness take over me for no apparent reason. I felt the same way when I met my birth mother, when I looked at my new babies, when I sat holding my adoptive mother's hand as she passed away. It's still there now, my familiar companion: I want to be acknowledged, I want Antonio to believe me, regardless of any tests.

I stand up and walk around my room. Suddenly I'm

overcome by a sudden urge to annihilate myself; it consumes me. I picture myself walking the streets of New York, looking for drugs. The pull to use is the strongest it has been in my many years of sobriety. In this moment, I want to destroy myself: the pain has gone on for too many years, I can't do it anymore – I'm feeling so much and for the first time I see the direct connection between my addiction and my adoption experience. I know I do have a choice, but I just want to get so out of my mind that I never have to feel any of this again. I'm so tired too.

I can't breathe. Somehow I manage to send a group text to some adoptee friends – I know if I don't reach out to someone, I'll hurt myself. I'm a mother, I have to think of my children.

'I want to use. I think I'm having a panic attack,' I manage to text.

My phone rings but I can't speak. I hear the gentle voice of Cathy, a fellow adoptee.

'Zara, you spent time with your father today. I know what it's like to be around our blood connection and feel a sense of familiarity that we've never had before. It's so joyous, but it brings up so much grief and pain.'

I have no words – I feel like I've burrowed down into my very core. Once I start crying, I can't stop. Cathy's so kind. She gets me to breathe and allows me to howl down the phone. Finally, I hear myself speak.

'I need him to know who I am – he had no idea I existed. All those years of wondering if he thought about me, I can't wait any longer. I know Pat is upset with me. I can't be in the middle again, protecting her from the harsh reality that he didn't remember her, that he didn't know about me; protecting his wife. I feel like I have to apologise for my existence – sorry, everyone, for being such an annoyance, a mistake. Sorry to my mum, for wanting to know my birth mother. Sorry, Dad, for needing to know my birth father. I'm so fucking tired of this fucking role! I can't do it anymore, I don't want to be a secret.'

I know I sound self–pitying, but I don't care.

'I want him to want me. I want him to shout from the rooftops about it, the way I want to. Is that too much to ask?'

I hear my friend laugh and I'm grateful. The desire to use drugs is passing and instead a fatigue has taken over. For the first time, I have reached out to people and let them see my deepest pain. How many times have I done this alone? I don't want to do it anymore.

The next morning, I'm out running errands when I check my phone and see that there's an email from the paternity test people: my results are in. I want to read it right now, but decide to wait until I'm home. I can't get home fast enough. I pull up to my house and charge upstairs.

I click on the link.

I'm scared, but I have to know.

Somebody's Daughter

Father: Antonio P. is not excluded as the biological
father. 99.9 percent.
Mother: Patricia G.
Baby: Zara Phillips.

It's him! It's really him. For the first time in my life, I see
all three of our names together on one page. All three of us
woven together, three strangers, connected. A deep sense of
relief washes over me.

23

My Father, 2016

'Hi, Antonio…' As promised, he is the first person I call. 'The results are in. You're my birth father.'

'Oh my God! I'm on the highway, I'll call you back.'

Moments later, he calls back.

'I had to pull over,' he explains. 'Life is indeed full of surprises! My wife, she's gonna kill me. I need some time to think. I will tell her, though. I promise, okay?'

'It's okay, I know you need time,' I say, not being totally honest. I want him to tell her, I don't want to be his secret.

'Zara, you know this is a shock, but I'm happy.'

My eyes instantly fill with tears; I'm thrilled.

'I am too, Antonio.'

Now I have to wait and let him do what he needs to do. I feel like all I do is wait for others to be ready to acknowledge my existence. After all these years, I just want to spend time with him. Already we've lost so much time together and I don't want to waste any more.

I haven't told my adoptive father about Antonio – I don't want to hurt him the way I hurt my mother. Does he need to know? Will it ruin the relationship it took us so many years to build? Would he be angry, or happy for me? I don't know, but I don't want to take that risk. I haven't spoken to my brother in two years. The last time I saw him we got in a fight so I've realised it is better that I keep my distance. I wish I could talk to a family member, but it doesn't feel safe.

Days are turning to weeks. Antonio phones, but all he has is excuses for why he hasn't told his wife about me yet. I try not to take it personally but the waves of emotion threaten to overwhelm me again. I try to stand as strong and tall as I can. I go to yoga and the gym; it makes me feel calmer. I surrender, accepting my powerlessness. I have to trust that this will play out the way it's meant to.

Michelle and I talk on the phone. We feel like twins separated at birth and I'm so grateful to know her.

'Zara, I'm coming to New Jersey next week. It's time we get him to take us to meet his wife,' she says.

I had broken down to her on the phone, the waiting getting to me again. I knew Antonio needed time, but I also knew he had a lot of shame: he might never tell her.

His wife, though, already suspected something was up.

She had texted Michelle to ask if there was another child out there. Michelle told her the truth; that we were waiting for confirmation. But I had confirmation now, there could be no more doubt.

So I tell Antonio that Michelle is coming and could we meet, but he continues to be scared. I urge him to try, as it could be the only time all three of us get together.

The morning Michelle is coming to New Jersey, she texts me: 'I'm so disappointed. It doesn't seem like he'll be in town, but at least we can spend time together.'

Five minutes later, my phone rings: it's him.

'Hi, so we're back from Connecticut. What's happening today?'

Stunned, I try my best to downplay it.

'I'm on my way to pick up Michelle and then we'll come and meet you. I'll call you from the car.'

I don't want to give him an excuse to not show up.

I pick up Michelle completely shaking at finally meeting her but amazed at how close I feel to her already, and we call our father from the car: 'Hello, Antonio! The girls are on their way.' We can hear him laugh nervously.

'You are both in the car?'

'Yes,' we reply in unison.

'Oh my God!' he says, laughing again. 'Okay, okay… Drive safely. See you soon. Dunkin' Donuts, okay?'

'Yes, Antonio, our favourite place.'

Somebody's Daughter

Michelle turns and says to me, 'You know, he just needs a little push, that's all. Today we have to get him to take you to meet his wife. She's lovely, I promise. We have to keep our eyes on the prize.'

'What would I do without you?' I say. I feel so incredibly grateful for her help – I don't think I would have the courage to do this alone.

We talk about another strange coincidence in the story of our reunion. A British adopted friend of mine, Nicole, has known Michelle's birth mother for years. A few years back, Nicole learnt that her friend was a birth mother and had reunited with her daughter, Michelle, who had recently met her father, Antonio. Nicole asked her friend if she thought it could possibly be the same man. Michelle remembered her mother telling her that another adopted person was looking for a man named Antonio, but she hadn't thought it could be possible.

'The adoption community in LA can't believe our story – we know all the same people.'

'I know, it's ridiculous. If I'd stayed in LA, we would have ended up sitting in a support group or a conference together,' I reply.

'No one put the pieces together, even though they knew we were both looking for a man with the same name – I think the accents threw them. How could we be related when we sound so different?'

'You can't make this stuff up, can you?'

* * *

As we pull into the Dunkin' Donuts car park, Antonio is already seated at a table, sipping his coffee. He looks so serious – we've never seen him like this before. We both try to lighten the mood by making jokes. I hand him the 'It's a Girl' balloon and he smiles.

'It's a girl alright,' he says.

'So,' Michelle says, getting straight to the point. She leans towards him and asks gently, 'Don't you think it's time to tell Lisa?'

'What, now?' He blinks.

'Yes,' she says. 'Let's all go and see her right now.'

I've been sitting quietly this whole time. Then I find myself saying to him, 'Just say, "Whoops, here's another one!"'

For some reason, it's broken the ice. Suddenly he can't stop laughing. He leans into me, tears in his eyes.

'You are such a crazy banana.'

Michelle and I look at one another, laughing with him at the absurdity of the situation.

'Okay, I will call her and tell her we're on our way.'

I'm seized by panic.

Antonio is yelling into the phone: 'Michelle's here, we're coming to the house! Yes, I know it's a surprise. I didn't know she was coming. Stop worrying about the bloody house! We'll be there in a minute.' We can hear a faint woman's voice shouting down the phone. He hangs up.

'Follow me.'

My nerves are at an all-time high. Michelle keeps me calm; she knows how I feel.

We follow him in my car; I see the balloon bobbing in the back of his car.

He is already parked as we pull in. Michelle gets out of the car and walks up to the front door, where Antonio is waiting. I linger awkwardly by the car.

Antonio waves me into the house. 'Get in the house. Go, go!'

I feel like my heart could stop at any moment. I'm led into a sitting room, where I wait by myself. I can hear a lady with a thick New Jersey accent shouting in the next room.

'I can't believe this! Why didn't you tell me you were coming? I would have prepared something. Antonio, put the vacuum away! Michelle, I'm a mess, don't look at me! Antonio, I'm going to kill you! Why do you do this to me?' I feel ready to run out of the house.

'Lisa, Lisa,' Michelle says quietly, 'it's okay. We have a surprise for you. Someone is here to meet you.'

There's dead silence. I'm frozen, unsure of what to do. Then a beautiful, petite woman with blonde hair is standing in front of me.

'Oh!' she says. 'Do you not live in Italy?'

She knew who I was straight away – she had suspected for weeks that there might be another child out there after overhearing a conversation with Michelle.

'No, I'm British and I live in New Jersey.' My voice is quiet. She stands for a moment, just looking at me.

'You're British? You live in New Jersey? Okay, *now* I'm shocked.'

She's clearly stunned. Then without any more hesitation, she walks over to me and gives me a warm hug. 'Welcome to the family! What's one more, eh?'

I'm so touched by her generous spirit as she ushers us to the table. As tea is being made, she pulls out the family photo albums, laying them on the table. Michelle takes photos of me: 'Watching you reminds me of me just a few years ago, sitting here doing the same thing.'

'You girls are lovely,' Lisa says, and then quietly to me, 'I knew there was another daughter – I overheard him talking on the phone. He is so ashamed. That's why he didn't tell me.'

As I sit looking at the photos, I feel completely overcome. I see pictures of all his sisters and brothers, his mother and father; I see myself in some of my aunts. I see my children in their children. I start to cry. I look up and Antonio has tears in his eyes.

'I want you to know I'm happy,' he says.

Somebody's Daughter

* * *

'I can't thank you enough,' I tell my new sister as we hug goodbye. 'If it wasn't for you, I would never have had the courage to push like this.'

'Even if we weren't sisters, I would still have wanted to be your friend. You know that, right?' she says.

That evening, I text Lisa to thank her for her kindness in accepting me into the family, fully aware not every woman would react like this.

'If I were adopted, I would want to know who my parents were. I'm so sorry you had to go through all of this.' she replies.

I feel so immensely happy. For them to acknowledge me was more healing than they could ever understand.

* * *

Just before Christmas, I invite Antonio and Lisa over to meet my daughters. Sadly, my son Samuel is away, so he won't get to meet them.

I notice how I'm still preparing myself for a rejection: what if Antonio cancels? When he calls to see how I am, I'm immensely happy. I know from experience that this is the typical roller-coaster ride adoptees can expect when they reunite with their birth family. Somehow, I thought that now I was older I would be able to handle it better. And in some ways, I can – I understand it more, but my emotions still sway back and forth like the tide.

I've even invited my ex-husband Kevin to meet Antonio. He's curious to meet the man I've been looking for all these years. I think back to the time he came with me to the Italian festival. He supported me as best he could during my outbursts and through my frustration. I'm glad that we get along much better now and he can come to the house. Antonio is here, and my girls are chatting with him and Lisa. The atmosphere is relaxed. He has brought along a briefcase of photos and is enjoying showing them off.

'That's all he does with his retirement, organise photos. He's thrilled to have someone so interested,' Lisa jokes to me.

I'm shocked by how closely I resemble one of his sisters. But why should it be strange that I look like my aunt? I know it's normal to look like a blood relative, but it's still so alien to me.

I watch Kevin talk to my birth father and I'm grateful for his interest, while feeling a tinge of sadness about how our relationship ended. *Was it all because of my divided identity?* I've thought about it a lot over the last three years. How could a couple who once loved each other so much end up unable to have a civil conversation? It still breaks my heart. I miss our family being a single unit, but I know this is best for both of us. And I wonder, why did I only meet Antonio now? Why not when I was still married? I think of the voice I heard that night, saying, 'It's all part of the bigger picture.'

I knew I was getting close.

24

Now

There is nothing sweeter in life than London at Christmas time. This year I'm visiting with all my children and I'm so excited. We're going to see my adoptive father for Christmas Eve, as well as my birth mother, my aunts and my nieces and nephews. I'm also going to meet one of my new brothers for the first time.

I had already spoken to this brother on the phone. Allessandro was Antonio's fourth child, the youngest, and he is a well-established artist in London. I'm thrilled that we have our love of the arts in common. He understands how I feel because he didn't get to grow up with his birth father either.

I'm glad I have my children with me as we make the long drive to his house. It's Boxing Day and Allessandro's whole family and his wife's family will be there too. As soon as he found out about my existence he was so supportive and so happy to have us come and meet everyone. I'm the surprise again, the stranger who happens to be his sister.

I'm nervous, joking with the kids that finally I don't have to meet a new family member on my own as we arrive at the house and Allessandro comes to the door. I feel awkward, unsure of what to say, but I'm immediately overwhelmed by his height, his handsome face; his eyes so much like mine. He welcomes us in and I notice how his whole family is staring: we look so much alike. We compare hands and features; we both realise how much we take after Antonio.

The day is perfect. We are all seated around a large kitchen table, the conversation flowing easily. The atmosphere is so warm and welcoming, I am overcome once more by the feeling of connection.

At the end of the day, I'm sad to leave them – I wish I could spend more time talking to my brother, but we need to go and see my dad. I'm still wondering whether or not to tell him about Antonio. I've lived my whole life burdened with secrets. I had lovers that no one could know about. I had family members that didn't know about me. I've kept secrets from my adoptive family. Even I was a secret… I feel weary from carrying them all.

When I see him, my father looks thinner. He's struggling to move around even more. I decide not to tell him. What's the point of telling him at this stage in his life? Do I want this for him, or for myself? I'm not sure anymore.

* * *

Late one evening, Cassie comes over to the house we are looking after in London while my friend is away. The kids are in their rooms, watching movies. We sit on the big sofa, cups of tea in hand.

'The whole thing is just so odd,' I tell her sleepily. 'I mean, think of all the men we've shagged!'

'Between us?' she says. 'I shudder with horror.'

'But that's what I mean. If we had ended up pregnant with one of them, we'd have no idea who the father was.'

'Probably not.'

'What I mean is, those liaisons weren't about love. They were because of lust, or alcohol.' My voice is pensive. 'I had wanted my conception to be something more than just two young people fooling around. When I hear other adopted people say their birth parents were madly in love, I almost feel jealous.'

'Why does that matter?' Cassie looks at me steadily.

'Because somehow I always knew I was a mistake. I've never felt like I had the same right to exist as everyone else. I know it sounds dramatic, but I feel like a second-class citizen, I just wanted to be the product of love.'

'Oh, Zara!' Cassie says earnestly. 'You have a life full of

love. Look at everything you have. I wish you knew how much the people in your life care about you.'

'I do, Cassie. At least, I'm finally beginning to."

'Then that has to be enough.'

* * *

I knew she was right: it was time to rid myself of the burden that I had carried for so long. I was loved; my life was full of it. The divorce had knocked the wind out of me, but I was finally ready to let it go. It was time to forgive myself for my mistakes. 'What's done is done', I had read recently. I had found those gentle words so comforting. I couldn't change what I had done in my marriage, all the mistakes I'd made: what was done was done.

Divorce is a lot like a death in the family. Yet instead of only remembering their good qualities the way we do when someone passes away, in divorce the beautiful memories become hidden. It's too painful to remember our family as it once was, whole and happy. But as I lay in the small, lumpy bed, I realised that if I kept punishing myself, I would never be able to allow those good memories to return. I needed to remember the good times, and so did my children.

As I fall asleep, a forgotten memory surfaces: Kevin and I are on the beach with the children. Samuel is about six, Katie and Anna a few years younger. We're all building a huge sandcastle. The waves are coming now, destroying parts of the beautiful home we have built. The more the waves come flooding in, the more furiously we work at keeping our house safe. How proud we all were that our castle survived while others hadn't. Back then we felt like we could survive anything, that we would always be protected. We held hands, singing and dancing around our sand home. I thought about how pretty the sky looked that day.

* * *

The next day, I stroll through the London streets to meet James and Terry. Samuel has taken his sisters to a museum, proud that he knows his way around London so well – we always make sure to meet up when I'm here. I meet up with them on Hampstead Heath. There are some kites flying high in the air, their colours dancing and colliding against the blue sky. We lie on our backs in the cold grass, talking about this and that. I'm grateful that we don't discuss anything too deep, I need a rest from heavy – it's fun to just be with them.

We watch three little girls playing. One of them stands with her arms open, while the other girl has her back to her. I can hear her yell, 'Now, do it now!' The girl falls back into her friend's waiting arms without fear or hesitation. They do this over and over. When it's the smallest girl's turn, she refuses.

'I can't, I just can't,' she says, on the verge of tears. 'What if no one's there to catch me? What if I fall?'

One of her friends puts her arm around her.

'I always hated those games, I could never let myself fall like that. I wish I could just pick that little girl up, she looks so sad,' I say.

James smiles at me gently.

'She'll figure it out.'

'I know,' I reply, 'it just takes time.'

'Look, Zara…' Terry is still looking in the children's direction.

I turn back to the group of kids. The little one is watching while the two older ones turn, run, jump and start falling forwards into each other's arms, laughing in delight.

I hear them say, 'Come on, Molly! You can do this.' I watch her pause, take a deep breath, then running forwards, she dives into their outstretched arms.

'You see? I told you she'd figure it out – we all do in the end.'

'It takes a lot longer for some, though,' I say ruefully.

'Especially you, Zara. You've taken years to sort through all your crap. Half a century now, isn't it?' Terry nudges me as we start to walk down the hill.

'Yes, Mr Wiseguy. Some of us are sicker than others. I've had you guys to walk the path with so no wonder it's taken me so bloody long! I'm just an extra-large onion. I have a lot of layers, and I'm okay with that.'

A couple of years back, James had finally met his

biological daughter. He had called me constantly during his search: 'Zara, was your father's name Judge S. Solomon?'

'Yes,' I answered, curious as to what he was going to say next.

'You're never going to believe it. Your father was the judge who oversaw my daughter's adoption.'

I couldn't speak; I felt a wave of nausea wash over me.

'Zara, you need to tell him he did the right thing. Her mother was an addict and I was an alcoholic – I couldn't take care of her at that time in my life. Zara,' he said quietly, 'your father saved my daughter's life.'

I'm so choked up, I can barely speak except to say: 'And you, dear James, saved mine.'

* * *

Tomorrow it's time to head back to New Jersey. We have had the most wonderful Christmas. I receive a lovely text from Allessandro and I find myself weeping in the car. I wonder what it would have been like to be raised with a little brother. I imagine him as a little boy and me as the protective older sister. I wonder what it would have felt like to grow up with brothers and sisters who were on my side, who cared about me, who didn't bully me. But that was not my childhood. I need to focus on what I have now. I'm an auntie to Pat's grandchildren. I love watching them grow up; I love being 'Auntie Wawa'. I get a chance now to be with family members who will always have known me. I cherish every moment with them.

Saying goodbye to my family is never easy, but for the first time I have a different feeling: I now have family in both Britain and America. I'm beginning to understand the path that the universe has laid out for me. I was always meant to come to America, I just never understood why until now.

In some ways, nothing has changed. I'm still split down the middle, part of two families. Having two sets of parents is complicated, but I can live with it.

Maybe living between two countries has been comfortable for me because the split life is something I already know. Divorce is a split life, too. Sometimes I wonder if I'll ever be able to live any other way – I find a strange sense of safety in it.

I continue to go to meetings and put my sobriety first. I have learnt that I will always have moments where my disease wants to lead me back down the path of self-destruction. But I owe everything I have today to my sobriety and I'm so grateful to the friends who supported me through it.

I go to an adoption group meeting in New Jersey each month to share experiences and really, to just hang out and have fun. I am now so grateful for this community who are always there for me. I feel so much more connected to this place now that I know my birth father lives here.

At first it's hard for Pat and my sister to adjust to me having found Antonio. They worry they will lose me. My adoptive mother had the same fear. Adoptees are always having to reassure our families our hearts are big enough for all of them.

My sister Michelle and I have had yet another revelation. We were looking back through old emails when she found one she had sent to me three years ago. We had somehow both forgotten about it. My friend Nicole, who knew her birth mother, had pushed her to contact me. We read the email:

Hello,

My name is Michelle. Cindy gave me your email address. She thinks we may have a connection through Antonio.

He's my birth father and he's from Rome. Cindy met him in the Channel Islands in 1966. I was born in November that year, and then put up for adoption.

I have spoken with Antonio but not met him. He lives in New Jersey. He is about 71 now. I don't know if he ever lived in London.

Somebody's Daughter

Is this helpful at all? Do you think there's any connection?

Best,
Michelle

We are both stunned. The only reason she remembered that she had sent it to me was that it came up on a thread in her emails. Four years ago, I had had his name right there in front of me. Four years ago, I first performed my one-woman show, *Beneath My Father's Sky*. The timing blows my mind. But three years ago, I was in a difficult place: I was about to get divorced. I understand now why I had to wait so long – it was indeed all part of a greater plan.

I often think about my adoptive mother. I still miss her so much it can physically hurt. I wonder what she would think about how my life has turned out. I feel that my relationship with my mother didn't die when she did, that it continues to grow. Her passing has allowed her to understand what I always needed: she helped me to complete my circle.

I had a clear memory the other day of how much I hated the dark when I was small. Maybe the darkness reminded me of what I didn't have. In the blackness I would strain the inside of my eyes to see their faces, but they were always moving – noses, eyes and mouths shifting, melting away before I could see them. My mother would hear me calling in the dark, a slight panic in my voice, to turn the hall light on and she would open my door halfway so I could sleep in the safety of the light.

* * *

Today is 29 January 2017. I'm driving home from Antonio's – I was invited for lunch with him and Lisa. It was the first time I had been back to the house since we surprised her a few months ago. Again, she welcomed me with open arms. Her generous heart stuns me. I spend the afternoon looking at photos of Antonio's family. Over the last year he has called me regularly and I still feel excited when I see his name come up on my phone. He is a kind, loving Italian man. His wife texts me to check in and share news. We have visited each other a few times. Slowly, we are figuring out how to make each other part of our lives. My new sister and brother and I are in touch. I still have yet to meet a few more siblings but I'm okay with it taking more time – my presence has been a surprise for everyone.

When I go to London I spend time with Pat and my siblings. I now have three nieces, who I love spending time with. I'm so happy that I am getting to see them grow up from birth.

My adopted father is now eighty-seven years old. We are both amazed that he outlived my mother by so many years and we joke that she would be as surprised as us. We continue to talk about Mum and we miss her. I gently tell Dad the work that I do within adoption, but I still protect him from my truth and I'm not exactly sure why. Maybe I'm still worried that he will reject me the way I was worried my mother would when she knew that I had found Pat.

I think of my mother's big suitcase full of family photos and how she would sit on the floor and show them to me. I believe that was her way of making me feel connected to the family. I loved to see them, but I never told her that I didn't really think of those people as my family, they were her family to me. I realise though that since I have found my birth family I can now feel more connected to my adopted family. The not knowing of my story left me feeling disconnected to everyone.

My birth family's acceptance and love for me has made my birth story so much easier to cope with. I think I'm finally shedding this core belief that I was not wanted and not meant to exist because I always thought of myself as a mistake. And when I look at my children they are my reminder how perfect they are, that no child born is ever a mistake.

As I drive, I run through a mental checklist. All three kids are thriving – they stretch out their wings more and more every day. My son and I have had an honest conversation about how we feel, and we're in touch a lot more. The love I have for these children continues to expand my heart. My ex-husband and I are getting along much better, although the grief still resurfaces sometimes. I can't deny that I still wish things had been different, but I'm grateful for what we have now. New and beautiful relationships are blossoming every day.

Many people have asked me over the last few months whether I feel whole now, complete. I find it hard to answer. All I know is I want to bathe in the energy of this new family. I feel more complete than I ever have before. Fully complete? I'm not sure as feelings of loss still rise to the surface. As I drive home, I sob the same way I did every time when I left my birth mother during those early meetings. I know it's just all part of the grief and joy of reunion, I know from experience these things take time; I also know that the feelings won't kill me.

For the first time in my life, I'm no longer searching: I have found. I know my story. I have seen their faces. I have heard their voices. I have been welcomed and embraced, and my heart feels still.

Acknowledgements

There are so many people to thank! I want to thank all my adoption peeps, who are so dear to my heart: the NJ care group, AAC – thank you, I adore you all. I would have to write another book to truly explain how you have all individually helped me. You are my soul family.

To my peeps: Sarah Elizabeth Greer, Tom McGee, David Petruzziello, Lisa Cooper, Kelly Ann, Kathy Coley, Kathy Costantino, Andrew Majkovich, Joe Pessolano, Pete Franklin, Judy Foster, Pam Hasagawa, Paula Monson, Nicole Burton, Lois Destefano, Pam Dixon Kroskie, Thomas Park Clement, Ron Nydam, Delores Tellor, Marilyn Waugh, William Kollar, Andrew Witt and Daryll McDaniels.

Thanks to Concerned United Birthparents: Mimi Janes, Karen Vedder, Trish Lay, Brian Stanton.

Somebody's Daughter

To Conram Baaf for publishing my first book, and particular thanks to Shaila Shar, Miranda Davis and Michelle Bell.

To Nicky Campbell for all your support and for writing the Foreword.

To Nimmy March.

To Marlou Russell for her wisdom and support.

To Lori Cooke and The Hyde School.

To Gabor Mate for all your support and wisdom.

To my wonderfully patient DNA search angel, Gaye Sherman Tannenbaum, who I know I drove crazy.

To Eliza and Eric Roberts, who directed my play, thank you for all your support and love over the years. To Keaton Simmons for the years of friendship.

To my dearest recovery friends, words do not express the gratitude and joy I feel for being lucky enough to trudge the road with you guys: Serena Roe, James Macaffrey, Terry Dove, Anita Nurse/Chellemah, Lisa Climie and Leslie Channon. To Paul Pickard (who I miss so much).

To my dear friend Penny Anderson for our daily talks and your encouragement and love.

To the Yanks in my life: my partner-in-crime Andrew Cohen, Elisa Stearn, William Kollar, Jimmy Ferrante, Marica Gloster Ammeen, Julie Jones, Diana Jones, Doug Feinstein, Elizabeth Rush, Carrie Cantor and Jane Schriener.

To Sandy Kugleman, I miss you.

To Lynne Oyama for all your support.

To the Brits in NJ. Yomi, Kofi, Michelle, Jemma and Deborah P.

To Melanie Redmond for the years being my singing sister and to Pete Briquette.

To my neighbours from childhood, my sisters, my friends, Katie Lachter, Roberta Rose and Debbie Roberts. Our street was insane but I never would have survived it without you all.

To Virginia Weissmuller, Janie Moore, Dani Medlin and Simon Hall for years of friendship.

To my fourth child Nina Sepal.

To Anna Ickowitz for your endless acceptance and love.

To Ronnie Paris, for the friendship and music.

To Richard Thompson for all your love and support. I'm so grateful you are in my life.

A special thank you to Bob Geldof for introducing me to Mark Cowne, and to Mark for not giving up on me and for setting up the meeting with Adrian Sington.

I would like to thank Adrian Sington for his support and encouragement for me completing this book and urging me, carefully and compassionately, to be as honest as I can.

To Bonnier and John Blake Publishing, and to my editor, Ciara Lloyd, for her patience and commitment to this book.

To my biological sister Roberta and brother Orlando,

and their beautiful children, Georgia, Sienna and Poppy who I so love being an aunt too – thank you for embracing me.

To my new American sister, Michelle: I am still so overwhelmed by the kind, gracious person you are. I feel like I won the jackpot!

Thank you to Allessandro and your wife and children, for opening your door to me and my children as soon as you knew about my existence.

To Antonio's wife, Lisa: how can I ever thank you for your open welcome arms? Your generosity has changed me.

To my ex-husband: thank you for making me a mother and being such a solid father for our beautiful children.

And of course to my babies, Zachary, Kayla and Arden. How do I put into words this kind of love? You have made my life – you fill my heart till it bursts with joy and pride.

To my birth mother, my birth father, my adoptive mother and my adoptive father: for being born and being raised, I thank you. I'm part of all of you, woven together in the finest threads.

This book is especially for anyone who has been touched by adoption: may your hearts be healed and your voices heard.

Helpful Information and Further Reading

Adoption UK – A national charity run by and for adopters

www.adoptionuk.org

Coram BAAF – Supporting agencies and professionals who work with children and young people

www.corambaaf.org.uk

* * *

Bond, Henrietta, *Control Freak, Losing Control* and *Remote Control* (2010, 2012, 2013)

> This series of hard-hitting novels for teenagers helps crack the stereotype of care leavers as feckless or hapless victims struggling to get their lives together.

Brodzinsky, '*Being Adopted, the Lifelong Search for Self*

Burton, Nicole, *Swimming Up the Sun*

Cairns, Kate and Brian, *Attachment, Trauma and Resilience* (2016)

> Another bestseller, this remarkable book uses the authors' personal

and professional experience to illuminate some of the realities of family life with children who have lived through overwhelming stress.

Campbell, Nicky, *Blue Eyed Boy*

Eldridge, S., *25 Things Adopted Kids Wish Their Adoptive Parents Knew*

Elliott, S., *Love Child: A Memoir of Adoption, Reunion, Loss and Love*

Fessler, Anne, *The Girls Who Went Away*

Harris, Perlita (ed.), *Chosen: Living with Adoption* (2012)

Thought-provoking writings by over 50 UK adopted adults born between 1934 and 1984.

Harris, Perlita (ed.), *In Search of Belonging* (2006)

A highly original anthology of poetry, prose, artwork, memoir and oral testimony that gives voice to over 50 transracially adopted children and adults.

Lifton, B.J., *Journey of the Adopted Self*

Lifton, B.J., *Lost and Found*

Mate, Gabor, *In the Realm of Hungry Ghosts*

Mulholland, James, *Special & Odd* (2007)

This revealing and witty memoir tells of how the author met his birth mother 29 years after being given up for adoption.

Pannor, Baron, Sorosky, *The Adoption Triangle*

Robinson, E. *Adoption and Loss*

Russell, Marlou, *Adoption Wisdom*

Schaefer, Carol, *The Other Mother*

Verny, Thomas, *The Secret Life of the Unborn Child*

Verrier, Nancy, *The Primal Wound* (2009)

Bestseller (first published in 1993) exploring the wound when a child is separated from her or his mother and the trauma this can cause.

All available from <u>corambaaf.org.uk/bookshop</u>